Design with Adobe® Creative Cloud

Basic projects using Photoshop®, InDesign®, Muse™, and more

CLASSROOM IN A BOOK®

The official training workbook from Adobe Systems

Adobe Press books are published by Peachpit, a division of Pearson Education located in San Francisco, California. For the latest on Adobe Press books, go to www.adobepress.com. To report errors, please send a note to errata@peachpit.com. For information on getting permission for reprints and excerpts, contact permissions@peachpit.com.

Writer: Conrad Chavez
Project Editor: Nancy Peterson
Development/Copyeditor: Anne Marie Walker
Production Editor: Katerina Malone
Technical Editor: Chad Chelius
Proofer: Darren Meiss
Compositor: Danielle Foster
Indexer: Karin Arrigoni
Cover design: Eddie Yuen
Interior design: Mimi Heft

Printed and bound in the United States of America

ISBN-13: 978-0-321-94051-3
ISBN-10:   0-321-94051-2

9 8 7 6 5 4 3 2 1

WHERE ARE THE LESSON FILES?

Purchasing this Classroom in a Book gives you access to the lesson files that you'll need to complete the exercises in the book, as well as other content to help you learn more about Adobe software and use it with greater efficiency and ease. The diagram below represents the contents of the lesson files directory, which should help you locate the files you need. Please see the Getting Started section for full download instructions.

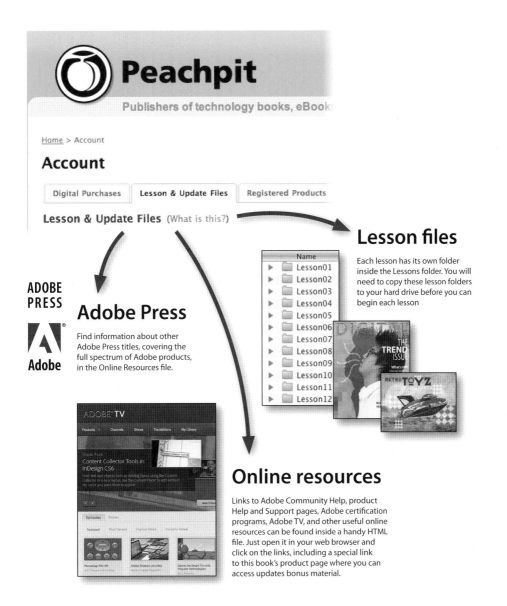

Adobe Press

Find information about other Adobe Press titles, covering the full spectrum of Adobe products, in the Online Resources file.

Lesson files

Each lesson has its own folder inside the Lessons folder. You will need to copy these lesson folders to your hard drive before you can begin each lesson

Online resources

Links to Adobe Community Help, product Help and Support pages, Adobe certification programs, Adobe TV, and other useful online resources can be found inside a handy HTML file. Just open it in your web browser and click on the links, including a special link to this book's product page where you can access updates bonus material.

CONTENTS

GETTING STARTED

Adobe Creative Cloud gives you everything you need to create your best work. With it you can deliver eye-catching digital images and graphics that remain crisp when scaled. You can also lay out high-impact printed pages with exquisite typography, build HTML5/CSS3 websites that look great on any screen, and design applications for tablets and smartphones.

This Classroom in a Book introduces you to the key elements and applications of Adobe Creative Cloud in a design workflow.

About Classroom in a Book

Design with Adobe Creative Cloud Classroom in a Book is part of the official training series for Adobe graphics and publishing software developed with the support of Adobe product experts. Each lesson in this book is made up of a series of self-paced projects that give you hands-on experience using the following Adobe products: Adobe Photoshop CC, Adobe Illustrator CC, Adobe InDesign CC, Adobe Muse CC, Adobe Acrobat XI Pro, and Adobe Bridge CC.

Design with Adobe Creative Cloud Classroom in a Book uses lesson files that are available online along with additional learning resources. To use these files, see "Accessing the Classroom in a Book files" later in this chapter.

Prerequisites

Before you begin working on the lessons in this book, make sure that you and your computer are ready.

Computer requirements

You'll need about 1.2 GB of free space on your hard drive to store all of the lesson files and the work files that you'll create as you work through the exercises.

Required skills

The lessons in this book assume that you have a working knowledge of your computer and its operating system. Make sure that you know how to use the pointer and the standard menus and commands, and also how to open, save, and close files. In addition, you should know how to use context menus, which open when you right-click/Control-click items, and scroll (vertically and horizontally) within a window to see content that may not be visible in the displayed area.

If you need to review these basic and generic computer skills, see the documentation included with your Microsoft Windows or Apple OS X software.

Installing Adobe Creative Cloud

Before you begin using *Design with Adobe Creative Cloud Classroom in a Book*, make sure that your system is set up correctly and that you've installed Adobe Creative Cloud. You must purchase an Adobe Creative Cloud subscription separately. For system requirements, see www.adobe.com/products/creativecloud/tech-specs.html#requirements.

Once you've begun your Creative Cloud subscription and installed the Creative Cloud desktop application, you can then install any of the software required for this book using the Apps tab in the Creative Cloud desktop app.

Because this book focuses on design, it does not use every Adobe Creative Cloud application. You need to install only the applications for the lessons you plan to complete.

Applications used in the lessons

	Lesson									
	1	2	3	4	5	6	7	8	9	10*
Adobe Bridge CC	•	•		•					•	•
Adobe Photoshop CC	•	•			•				•	•
Adobe Illustrator CC	•									
Adobe InDesign CC		•				•	•	•	•	•
Adobe Acrobat Pro XI		•						•		
Adobe Muse CC			•	•						

* Lesson 10 is available online from peachpit.com along with the downloadable lesson files for this book (see "Downloading the Classroom in a Book files").

Downloading the Classroom in a Book files

To work through the projects in this book, you'll need to download the lesson files from peachpit.com. You can download the files for individual lessons, or download them all at one time.

To access the Classroom in a Book files:

1   On a Mac or PC, go to www.peachpit.com/redeem and enter the code found at the back of your book.

2   If you do not have a Peachpit.com account, you will be prompted to create one.

3   The downloadable files will be listed under the Lesson & Update Files tab on your Account page.

4   Click the lesson file links to download them to your computer.

5   Any ZIP files you download are compressed, so double-click to decompress them before beginning the lessons. When decompressed, they will appear as folders containing lesson files.

Checking for Updates

Adobe periodically provides software updates. To check for updates in any program, go to the Help menu and choose Updates. For book updates and bonus material, visit your Account page on Peachpit.com.

Additional Resources

Design with Adobe Creative Cloud Classroom in a Book is not meant to replace documentation that comes with the program or to be a comprehensive reference for every feature. Only the commands and options used in the lessons are explained in this book. For comprehensive information about program features and tutorials, please refer to these resources:

Adobe Creative Cloud Help and Support: At helpx.adobe.com/creative-cloud/topics/getting-started.html you can find and browse Help and Support content on adobe.com.

Adobe Creative Cloud Learning: helpx.adobe.com/creative-cloud/tutorials.html provides inspiration, key techniques, cross-product workflows, and updates on new features. The Creative Cloud Learn page is available only to Creative Cloud members.

Adobe Forums: forums.adobe.com lets you tap into peer-to-peer discussions, questions and answers on Adobe products.

Adobe TV: tv.adobe.com is an online video resource for expert instruction and inspiration about Adobe products, including a How To channel to get you started with your product.

Adobe Design Center: www.adobe.com/designcenter offers thoughtful articles on design and design issues, a gallery showcasing the work of top-notch designers, tutorials, and more.

Adobe Developer Connection: www.adobe.com/devnet.edu.html is your source for technical articles, code samples, and how-to videos that cover Adobe developer products and technologies.

Resources for educators: www.adobe.com/education.edu.html includes three free curriculums that use an integrated approach to teaching Adobe software and can be used to prepare for the Adobe Certified Associate exams.

Also check out these useful links:

Adobe Marketplace & Exchange: adobeexchange.com is a central resource for finding tools, services, extensions, code samples, and more to supplement and extend your Adobe products.

Adobe Creative Cloud home page: creative.adobe.com is the page where you can sign into Creative Cloud, so that you can gain access to Creative Cloud services and application downloads.

Adobe Labs: labs.adobe.com gives you access to early builds of cutting-edge technology, as well as forums where you can interact with both the Adobe development teams building that technology and other like-minded members of the community.

Adobe Certification

The Adobe training and certification programs are designed to help Adobe customers improve and promote their product-proficiency skills. There are four levels of certification:

• Adobe Certified Associate (ACA)

• Adobe Certified Expert (ACE)

• Adobe Certified Instructor (ACI)

• Adobe Authorized Training Center (AATC)

The Adobe Certified Associate (ACA) credential certifies that individuals have the entry-level skills to plan, design, build, and maintain effective communications using different forms of digital media.

The Adobe Certified Expert program is a way for expert users to upgrade their credentials. You can use Adobe certification as a catalyst for getting a raise, finding a job, or promoting your expertise.

If you are an ACE-level instructor, the Adobe Certified Instructor program takes your skills to the next level and gives you access to a wide range of Adobe resources.

Adobe Authorized Training Centers offer instructor-led courses and training on Adobe products, employing only Adobe Certified Instructors. A directory of AATCs is available at partners.adobe.com.

For information on the Adobe Certified programs, visit training.adobe.com/certification.html.

ADOBE CREATIVE CLOUD

Everything you need to create your best work

Creative work crosses more boundaries than ever. Projects can be cross-media, possibly destined for print, web, and video. They can be cross-platform, appearing on computers, tablets, and smartphones. And they can be collaborative, with team members spread across cities or countries.

Access to the entire collection of Creative Cloud tools helps you solve any creative problem. Solutions such as Adobe Digital Publishing Suite, Single Edition and Adobe Muse greatly simplify publishing content on new media platforms. Take advantage of the Creative Cloud website (creative.adobe.com) and integration with the Behance creative community to easily share your work with project colleagues or potential clients.

Adobe Creative Cloud helps you meet your workflow challenges by providing you with the tools to create, work together, share, and publish.

Create professional graphics and type

A design project typically involves many components, including images, drawings, text, interactivity, and dynamic media, such as video and audio. Creative Cloud brings together graphics, type, and color tools that you can use to create or edit a wide range of media for any creative project.

Edit images precisely with Photoshop CC

Adobe Photoshop CC offers more speed, power, and freedom to create compelling images as the standard in professional, image editing software. You can start from a digital camera image and create digital paintings with flexible brush tools or graphics for websites. You can also use intelligent editing tools to create composite images by combining elements, correct lens curvatures and other distortions, create photographic blur effects, straighten images in seconds, create 360-degree panoramas, extend depth of field, and more.

Adobe Camera Raw 8, included with Photoshop CC, lets you edit the raw formats of many digital cameras and provides improvements that help you heal images, fix perspective distortions, and create vignettes. In addition, in Photoshop CC, Adobe Camera Raw is available as a filter you can apply to any layer.

Photoshop includes robust Save for Web tools for optimizing your images for any medium, from print to online to mobile. You can share images directly from Photoshop to Behance so you can showcase your work or get feedback from colleagues.

Because digital video has become an essential part of many creative projects, you can use Photoshop to edit video with a designer-friendly user interface. You'll edit a video in Photoshop in Lesson 5, "Creating a Video with Photoshop."

Create scalable designs and drawings with Illustrator CC

When you want to create drawings, designs, logos, and patterns that scale easily as vector graphics, Adobe Illustrator CC provides a deep set of tools so you can develop ideas quickly and precisely. You can use Image Trace to convert photos or other images into vector artwork, create smooth-edged shapes using precise drawing tools, or paint with brush strokes you can edit. The type tools in Illustrator support advanced typography, and you can develop logos and other designs based on font characters you've converted to paths.

The ability to create multiple artboards of different sizes lets you work out multiple variations or iterations of your design projects in a single Illustrator document. For example, you can design a set of business stationery that includes a business card, letterhead, and envelope, and store them all in the same Illustrator file.

As in Photoshop, you can prepare your Illustrator graphics for the web or mobile devices using Save for Web optimization tools, and you can share your Illustrator projects directly to Behance for self-promotion or feedback.

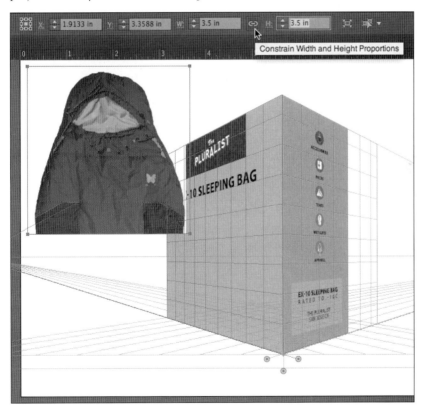

Gain access to thousands of fonts with TypeKit

Note: As this book is being written, Adobe plans to let you use TypeKit fonts with any of your desktop applications by syncing them to your desktop. For the current status of this feature, check your Creative Cloud desktop app for updates: This app will be used to enable the desktop font sync feature.

Your Creative Cloud subscription gives you access to thousands of valuable fonts through Adobe TypeKit, making it much easier and faster for you to find the perfect font. You can use Adobe TypeKit fonts directly from Adobe Muse.

Create color schemes with Adobe Kuler

Adobe Kuler lets you create color themes in some Creative Cloud applications, using an iPhone or using your web browser. The Adobe Kuler iPhone app lets you capture color schemes from whatever is in front of you (such as a garden or a street scene), or you can design your own color scheme using the Kuler app or website (kuler.adobe.com). You can use Creative Cloud to sync your Kuler color schemes between Creative Cloud applications, the Kuler website, and Adobe apps. The Kuler website is also a great place to explore color themes shared by others.

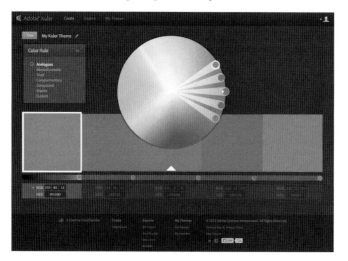

Design publications for print and mobile devices

Once you have completed the components for your design projects, you need to integrate them into a finished, polished piece. Creative Cloud provides the essential pieces that complete your design workflow.

Create print and online documents with Adobe InDesign CC

As a hub for publication design and production, InDesign is where everything comes together: With InDesign, you can lay out pages that include content, such as images from Adobe Photoshop CC, scalable artwork from Adobe Illustrator CC, and styled text from your word processor. You can create documents many pages long that remain easy to maintain and revise thanks to production-strength tools for text and graphics.

With deep roots in high-end print publishing, the powerful and precise layout features in InDesign help you meet the highest professional standards of creative design, typography, production, and final output. The sophisticated layout capabilities in InDesign now drive digital publishing—from fast and efficient output of PDF files and EPUB ebooks to the ability to work directly with Adobe Digital Publishing Suite to create book apps for tablets and smartphones. Liquid Layout rules, Alternate Layouts, Linked Content, and the Content Collector greatly simplify creating and maintaining layouts for multiple devices from one publication.

Produce professional-quality PDF files with Adobe Acrobat XI Pro

Adobe Creative Cloud includes Adobe Acrobat XI Pro because the Adobe Portable Document Format (PDF) plays a central role in many design workflows. With Adobe Acrobat XI Pro, you can create and edit professional PDF files for delivery of print design projects for final output on press, and for sharing and distributing documents or interactive titles online.

Although Creative Cloud applications such as InDesign, Illustrator, and Photoshop make it easy to create full-featured interactive or press-ready PDF files on their own, Acrobat XI Pro is valuable when you want to perform further enhancement, management, and optimization, such as combining multiple PDF files and reducing the file size of the combined file.

If you design print publications, Acrobat XI Pro integrates smoothly with the print production features in Adobe InDesign CC, such as color management and CMYK support, and with long document features, such as a hyperlinked index and table of contents. If you create online documents for desktop or mobile devices, you can use Acrobat Pro to design interactive forms, protect sensitive information, add media (such as video and audio), and include multiple types of materials in one file. You can also organize and track online reviews of shared documents and collect comments.

Share work with your community

Design is typically a collaborative activity between designer, client, and community, and that collaboration increasingly happens online. Adobe Creative Cloud supports online collaboration through features such as the Behance online creative community and file syncing.

Get connected with Behance

Adobe Creative Cloud gives you direct access to the Behance creative community where you can showcase your work, get feedback, and find creative inspiration. Behance provides you with a way to reach out beyond your local community and connect with top creatives around the world.

Creative Cloud applications streamline your connection to Behance. Instead of having to switch to a web browser to work with Behance, you can upload your work directly from applications, such as Adobe Photoshop CC and Adobe Illustrator CC, and you can monitor your Behance activity stream directly in the Creative Cloud desktop app. You can display your work publicly or to a specific audience and get

Note: As this book is being written, Adobe plans to integrate Behance with more Creative Cloud applications. For the current status of this feature, check your Creative Cloud desktop app for application updates. Applications integrated with Behance have a Share on Behance command (File > Share on Behance).

the feedback you need to improve your work. Behance includes direct connections to social media like Twitter and Facebook to help you promote your work online.

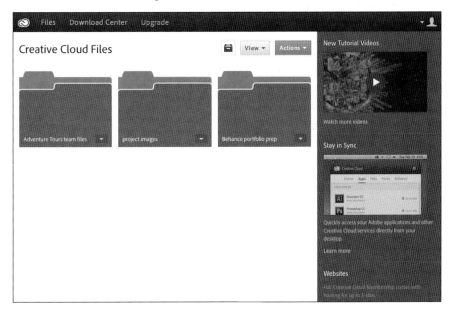

Privately share files with Creative Cloud online storage

Your Adobe Creative Cloud account provides you with online file storage and sharing. You can upload and share files through a web browser. Storing files online makes it easier for you to work anywhere, and the ability to share files privately makes Creative Cloud storage useful for collaboration.

Note: As this book is being written, Adobe plans to let you synchronize files on your desktop with Creative Cloud online file storage so that you don't have to manually upload and download them. For the current status of this feature, check your Creative Cloud desktop app for updates.

Create customized websites for your work or clients

Sharing your work on your own website is essentially required in today's design world, but building a website can require skills, time, and energy that draw you away from your creative projects. Adobe Creative Cloud provides several ways to create personalized websites without writing code, depending on what you need.

Show your best work in a ProSite portfolio

You can create a professional public portfolio easily and quickly using ProSite, a pro-level feature of Behance. In ProSite, portfolio creation begins by selecting a layout, customizing it, and adding projects. ProSite includes beautiful templates and powerful controls for personalizing the look of your portfolio, all within your web browser. When you're ready to show your work to the world, click Publish. This example shows a portfolio containing one project; to see real-world examples of portfolios with many projects you can explore, visit www.behance.net.

You can link your Behance account to other social network accounts, including Twitter, LinkedIn, Google, and Facebook, so that it just takes an instant to promote any of your content from Behance. As you grow your Behance ProSite presence, you can monitor its effectiveness with built-in statistics reporting that includes project views and portfolio views over time.

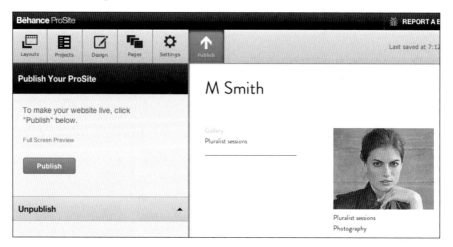

Build your own website in Adobe Muse CC without writing code

If you want to create a fully customized website design, you can do it in Adobe Muse CC without writing code. Adobe Muse stands out from other website creation tools in that you can design websites using familiar tools and commands like those in Adobe InDesign CC. You can create your website by thinking like a designer, not a web programmer.

The design freedom Muse provides doesn't compromise the technical quality of the site. Websites you create with Muse adhere to web standards, and you can easily create a single site with layouts customized for desktop computers, tablets, and smartphones. When you create mobile versions of a website, not only are they sized appropriately for the screen, but they also respond to touch gestures like swipes and pinches. These advantages help provide your site's visitors with a positive experience, no matter how they view your site.

Adobe Creative Cloud also simplifies publishing and hosting of your website by providing you with Adobe Business Catalyst web hosting services. Your Creative Cloud subscription lets you use Business Catalyst to host up to five websites for you or your clients.

You'll work with an Adobe Muse website in Lesson 3, "Creating a Mobile-Friendly Website."

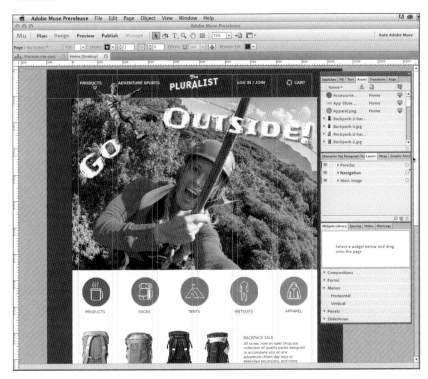

Work flexibly, online or offline

Adobe Creative Cloud works for you whether or not you are connected to the Internet. When you're connected to the Internet, you can take advantage of application integration with Creative Cloud online tools. You can continue to work when you aren't online because Creative Cloud applications are installed locally on your computer. You can store your files locally (on your own disks or servers) or in the online storage provided as part of your Creative Cloud account.

Manage project files using Adobe Bridge

With Adobe Bridge CC, you can manage your media with centralized access to all of your creative assets. Regardless of the Adobe Creative Suite software you use, your projects will likely involve various files and formats. You may be organizing documents and graphics from different sources or finding your way through a large media library. Adobe Bridge is an advanced media manager that helps you quickly locate and organize the files you need, and move them directly into the Adobe Creative Suite software you're using. Adobe Bridge helps you work with images, text, the native file formats of Creative Suite software—such as Photoshop, InDesign, and Illustrator—videos, fonts, and more. Powerful searching, content filters, and thumbnail views help you zero in on the files you need, and large previews enable you to ensure that you're opening the correct file. You'll use Adobe Bridge in many lessons in this book.

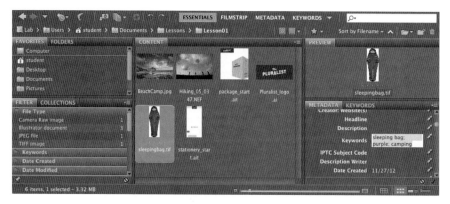

Take your work anywhere

When you're away from your computer, you can work on any other computer that meets the system requirements for Creative Cloud. Your subscription works on up to two computers, such as a desktop and a laptop, or even one Mac and one Windows computer. For example, you can work on a computer at a client's office by signing into Creative Cloud, downloading the applications you need, and then signing out when you're done. This flexible licensing also makes it easy to stay on schedule on a secondary computer if your primary computer is out for repairs.

To save even more time, you can synchronize the settings of some applications to Creative Cloud. For example, you can sync Photoshop preferences, actions, brushes, and other settings to Creative Cloud. This makes it easy to set up your Photoshop customizations on another computer or to quickly restore your personal settings in case you have to reinstall Photoshop.

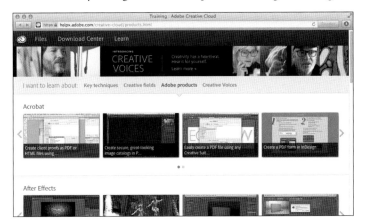

If you upload your project files to the online storage included with your Creative Cloud subscription, you'll be able to download those files on another computer. Combined, the flexible licensing, settings synchronization, and online file storage give you the ability to liberate your work from your primary computer so you can complete it anywhere.

Get more training anytime

With all of the tools available to you through Creative Cloud, you'll sometimes want to use an application or service that's new to you. An extensive library of Creative Cloud training videos help you get up and running quickly when you encounter a Creative Cloud tool that's unfamiliar. Immediate access to relevant training helps save time that you might otherwise spend searching for the right tutorial.

▶ **Tip:** To watch additional training videos about Adobe applications, visit tv.adobe.com.

Expand your creative universe

Although you might initially use the Adobe Creative Cloud applications that focus on design, Creative Cloud gives you plenty of room to grow as you develop your career.

Photography

If you routinely work with photo shoots using Adobe Camera Raw, Adobe Photoshop, and Adobe Bridge, you might consider using Adobe Photoshop Lightroom. It's optimized for precise processing and highly efficient organization of large numbers of photos and lets you easily create slide shows, videos, and books from your photographs.

Video editing and production

You can quickly create a video using the designer-friendly video-editing tools in Photoshop CC, as you will in Lesson 5, "Creating a Video with Photoshop." If you feel like tackling more ambitious video projects, Creative Cloud provides professional video production tools as well, such as Adobe Premiere Pro CC, Adobe After Effects CC, Adobe Audition CC, and Adobe SpeedGrade CC.

Web development

Although ProSite and Adobe Muse are the best options for building websites if your focus is on design rather than coding, experienced web programmers can take advantage of a variety of advanced Adobe Creative Cloud web development tools, including Adobe Dreamweaver CC, Adobe Flash Professional CC, Edge Code CC, Edge Inspect CC, and Edge Reflow CC.

Touch App plug-ins

If you use Adobe Touch Apps such as Photoshop Touch or Adobe Ideas on your smartphone or tablet, you can integrate them with Creative Cloud desktop apps using Touch App plug-ins. For example, by installing Touch App plug-ins, you can transfer an image you edited using Photoshop Touch from your tablet to Photoshop CC on your desktop. You can install the Touch App plug-ins from the Creative Cloud desktop app.

Let's begin

Now that you've been introduced to the full range of applications and services that Creative Cloud offers, it's time to jump into Lesson 1 and start learning about the Creative Cloud tools that will enhance your design workflow.

1 CREATING VISUAL IDENTITY MATERIALS

Lesson overview

The way you set up your documents and create your assets will affect how easily and efficiently you can design your work. This lesson will introduce you to some important skills and concepts:

- Organizing your work in Adobe Bridge
- Creating a coordinated set of stationery, an envelope, and a business card
- Creating a background image for a social media website
- Setting up multiple Illustrator artboards to contain a project in a single document
- Drawing in perspective in Illustrator CC
- Tracing an image in Illustrator CC
- Cropping a photo in Photoshop CC

 You'll probably need between one and two hours to complete this lesson. Download the project files for this lesson from the Lesson & Update Files tab on your Account page at www.peachpit.com and store them on your computer in a convenient location, as described in the "Getting Started" section of this book. Your Accounts page is also where you'll find any updates to the chapters or to the lesson files. Look on the Lesson & Update Files tab to access the most current content.

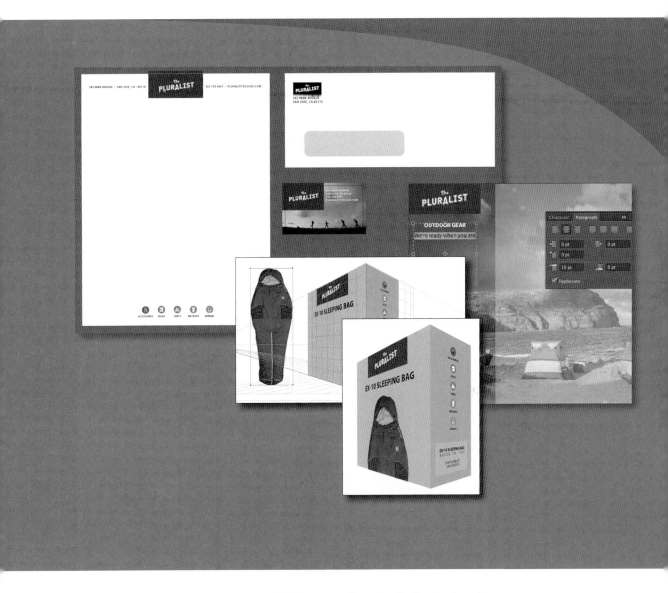

In this lesson, you'll use Creative Cloud software to design a visually coordinated set of materials for a business and a background for the same business's profile on a social media website.

Note: If you have not already downloaded the project files for this lesson to your computer from your Account page, make sure you do so now. See "Getting Started" at the beginning of the book.

Organizing your work with Adobe Bridge

In this lesson, you'll be working in Adobe Bridge CC, Adobe Illustrator CC, Adobe Photoshop CC, and Adobe Acrobat Pro.

Adobe Bridge CC provides integrated, centralized access to your project files and enables you to quickly browse through your creative assets visually—regardless of what format they're in—making it easy for you to locate, organize, and view your files.

Adding folders to your Favorites

To help you access your files easily, Adobe Bridge adds your Pictures and Documents folders (Mac) or your My Pictures and My Documents folders (Windows) to the Favorites panel by default. You can add as many of your frequently used applications, folders, and documents as you like to the Favorites panel. In the Preferences dialog box for Adobe Bridge you can even specify which of the default favorites you want to keep in the Favorites panel.

After you've copied the Lessons folder from your Account page at www.peachpit.com to your computer, it's a good idea to add your Lessons folder to the Favorites panel in Adobe Bridge, so that the files you'll use for the lessons in this book will be only a click away. You could also add your Lesson01 folder right below that and keep it there while you work through this lesson.

Tip: You can also quickly add a folder to your Favorites by right-clicking/Control-clicking the folder in the Content panel and choosing Add To Favorites from the context menu.

1   Start Adobe Bridge CC. At the top of the Adobe Bridge window, make sure the Essentials workspace is selected.

2   Navigate to your Lessons folder, and then select the Lesson01 folder in the Content panel. Drag it into the list in the Favorites panel in the left panel group, taking care not to drop it inside another folder.

Tip: If you can't read all your filenames or the thumbnail images are not big enough, you can enlarge them by using the Zoom slider near the bottom-right corner.

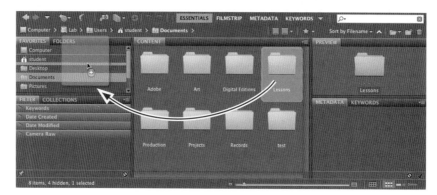

Having your Lessons files easily accessible will save you a great deal of time as you work your way through the lessons in this book.

Adding metadata

All your documents contain some metadata, such as information about the device with which they were created. You can use Adobe Bridge to add your own metadata to a single file or to multiple files at the same time—without having to open the application specific to those files.

In this first exercise you'll see how easy it is to add metadata to a file and learn some different ways to mark it, which will make it easier to find and sort.

1   In Adobe Bridge, navigate to your Lesson01 folder to see the files inside. You'll be working with these files later in this lesson.

2   Select the file sleepingbag.tif and note the Metadata panel in the right panel group.

3   In the Metadata panel, expand the IPTC Core panel, and type **sleeping bag, purple, camping** in the Keywords text field.

You just entered three keywords, using a comma to separate them so they are entered individually. You can also enter keywords using the Keywords panel that you may see grouped with the Metadata panel. But when you're entering many types of metadata, you may find it more convenient to enter them in the Metadata panel along with everything else.

4   Click the Apply check mark in the bottom-right corner of the Metadata panel to apply your entries.

Tip: You can't apply keywords by pressing the Enter/Return key because that creates a new line in the Keywords field. However, if your keyboard has a numeric keypad, you can apply the keywords by pressing the Enter key there (or by pressing Fn+Enter on most keyboards without numeric keypads).

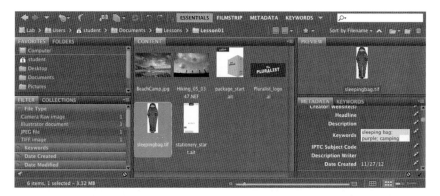

Tip: Keywords you enter are searchable in the search field in the top-right corner of an Adobe Bridge window, as well as in Mac OS X Spotlight and Windows Desktop Search. They can also be preserved when exporting versions of the images to share online.

When you search for this file in the future, the metadata you just added will help you find this specific file. Adobe Bridge looks in the metadata fields when you search for a file in Adobe Bridge, and in addition, the search features built into Microsoft Windows and Mac OS X also look for keywords to improve their search results.

Tip: The panel arrangements in this book are based on how each application looks when first installed. If you've moved your panels, you can return them to the default positions by choosing Reset Workspace from the workspace menu in the application.

Marking your files with ratings and color labels

When you're working with a large number of files and folders, assigning ratings and labels is a good way to mark a large number of files quickly, making it easier to sort and find them later.

1   In the Content panel, note the five dots above the filename sleepingbag.tif, indicating that this file has not yet been rated. Click the third dot, which will apply a three-star rating—it's that easy to rate a file.

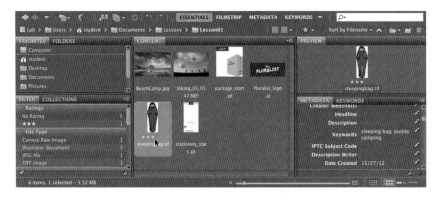

You can also mark a file visually by assigning a color label.

2   Choose Label > Approved. Your file is marked with a green color label, which you can also see in the Preview panel.

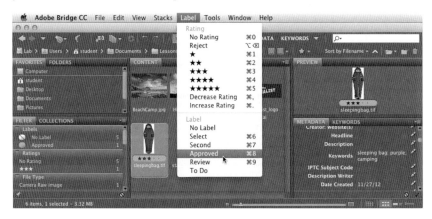

Tip: You can customize Label names and colors in the Preferences dialog box.

This color labeling system is not only useful to help you quickly spot the images you're looking for, but is also an effective way to sort your images by category, production status, or any other meanings you assign to the labels. This can be an effective organizational tool, especially when different people are working on the same project. You can use the Filter panel to quickly locate files with specific ratings or labels.

3 Right-click/Control-click the sleeping bag image, and choose Sort > By Label from the context menu. If you had multiple files with the same label, they would now be grouped in the Content panel. You can change the sort order by toggling View > Sort > Ascending Order.

▶ **Tip:** You can also control sort criteria and order at the right side of the path bar.

Synchronizing color management

Using Adobe Bridge as your central hub enables you to synchronize the color management settings across the Creative Cloud applications that support Adobe color management settings. It's highly recommended to use this feature to help ensure that colors are consistent, especially in the workflows discussed in Chapter 10, "Managing Color Across Adobe Creative Cloud."

A range of options are available for synchronizing color management. You can specify your own color settings in the Color Settings dialog box in the relevant Adobe application, and then apply it to all the other Adobe Creative Cloud applications in Adobe Bridge, or you can choose one of the Adobe Bridge presets.

1 In Adobe Bridge, choose Edit > Color Settings.

2 The Color Settings dialog box appears. A message at the top of the dialog box tells you whether or not the settings are already synchronized. If they are not, click North America General Purpose 2 in the Color Settings list, and then click Apply. If the Apply button isn't active, select any setting, and then select North America General Purpose 2 and click Apply.

The next time you open the Color Settings dialog box, the message at the top of the dialog box should now indicate that your Creative Cloud applications use the same color management settings.

Creating business stationery in Adobe Illustrator CC

A basic set of business stationery typically includes standard-size sheets for correspondence, envelopes, and business cards. These pieces must use a consistent, coordinated design, and yet they are all different sizes. You can easily manage such a project in Adobe Illustrator CC, which supports multiple artboards, each of which can be a different size.

Working with multiple artboards

In Illustrator CC, you can work with up to 100 different artboards in a single file. You can control the size of the artboards as well as the spacing in between them. Multiple artboards can be named and organized in rows and columns, and can be printed, exported, and saved separately.

Being able to have several artboards within one file suits the way most designers work: Usually, numerous iterations of a design concept are necessary to arrive at the polished final version, and a designer will often work on multiple pieces that are related.

Note: If a dialog appears saying "Settings from another computer are already synced with Creative Cloud," click Disable Sync Settings for now. If you want to sync settings later, you can do so by opening the Illustrator Preferences dialog box and clicking Sync Settings.

1   In your Lesson01 folder, double-click the file stationery_start.ai.

    This file contains two artboards arranged vertically. You may not be able to see them both right away.

2   Choose View > Fit All in Window (Ctrl-Alt-0/Command-Option-0). Now you can see all artboards at once.

3   Choose File > Save As, and make sure you save the file as stationery.ai in the Lesson01 folder.

4 Click Save, and in the Illustrator Options dialog box that appears, click OK.

The larger artboard is a stationery design, and the smaller artboard is an envelope. Red lines around each artboard indicate the bleed area, the area where the design extends beyond the edge of the page. After each piece is printed, the bleed area is trimmed so that design elements cleanly meet the edge of the paper. The same bleed amount applies to all artboards in the document.

Cyan lines within each artboard are ruler guides that were added by the designer to indicate areas close to the edge that text or critical design elements should avoid because there is a chance they may be trimmed after printing. You'll work with guides later in this lesson.

5 Select the Artboard tool () (press Shift-O), and click the envelope artboard to select it.

Tip: When you create a new Illustrator document, you can specify the number of artboards you want and their size, position, and spacing in the New Document dialog box.

Tip: If you want to see or change the bleed amount, choose File > Document Setup.

Tip: In the Envelope design, the rounded rectangle represents a cutout in the paper (not a printed area), so it's on a nonprinting layer.

The Control panel updates to present artboard options; this is where you can set the size, orientation, and name of the selected artboard.

You can freely arrange artboards; they don't have to be perfectly aligned. In this case, the two artboards will fit better on the screen if arranged horizontally.

6   Choose View > Guides and make sure that Lock Guides is deselected. If Lock Guides is selected, the guides won't move with the artboard in step 8.

7   In the View menu, make sure Smart Guides is selected.

8   Using the Artboard tool, drag the envelope artboard to the right of the first artboard, positioning it so that the top edges of both artboards are aligned; release the mouse when a green Smart Guide appears horizontally to confirm alignment.

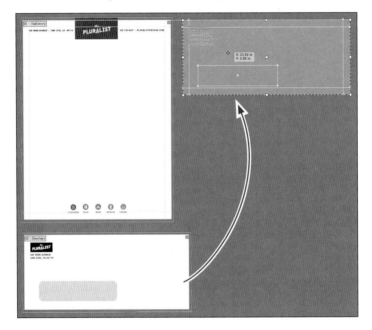

Smart Guides help you align objects quickly because they appear only when you need them, and automatically disappear when you're done in order to minimize visual clutter.

9 Choose View > Fit All in Window to fit the new arrangement of artboards into the document window.

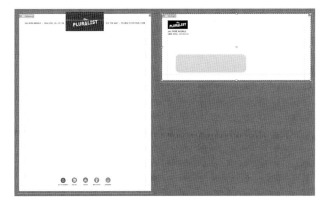

10 Choose File > Save.

Add a new artboard

You'll now add a business card to this document by adding another artboard.

1 Position the Artboard tool just below the bottom-left corner of the envelope; a Smart Guide should appear when you've aligned the pointer with the left edge of the envelope.

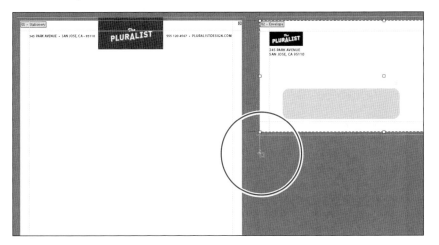

Note: If you release the mouse but the artboard is not the correct size, you can easily edit the size. With the artboard still selected, edit the W and H values in the Control panel to read 3.5 inches and 2 inches, respectively.

2 Drag right and down to create a new artboard 3.5 inches wide and 2 inches tall. The measurement label that appears by the pointer precisely indicates the artboard size as you drag. If you have trouble achieving the exact measurement, zoom in for more precision.

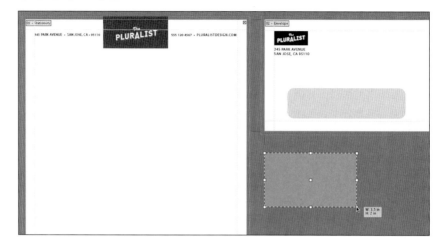

3 In the Control panel, enter **Business Card** as the Name.

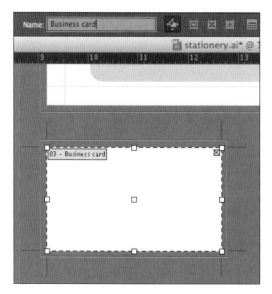

Now you'll add four guides to indicate the safe area for type and important graphics. You can create two kinds of guides in Illustrator: global guides and artboard guides. Global guides appear across all artboards, and artboard guides exist only on a specific artboard. You'll create artboard guides for the business card so that they don't affect the other artboards, but first you'll change the ruler origin so that it's relative to the business card.

4 Position the Artboard tool over the intersection of the horizontal and vertical rulers, and drag the ruler origin to the top-left corner of the Business Card artboard.

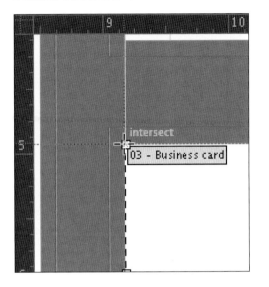

5 Position the Artboard tool over the horizontal ruler and drag a guide from the ruler down to the Business Card artboard; release the mouse when the guide reaches 3/16" on the vertical ruler.

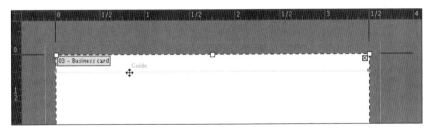

6 Add another horizontal ruler guide to the Business Card artboard at 1 13/16" on the vertical ruler.

7 Position the Artboard tool over the vertical ruler and drag a guide to the right from the ruler to the Business Card artboard; release the mouse when the guide reaches 3/16" on the horizontal ruler.

▶ Tip: To snap a guide to ruler increments as you create it, hold down Shift as you drag the guide.

8 Add another vertical ruler guide to the Business Card artboard at 3 5/16" on the vertical ruler.

9 Choose File > Save.

The guides remained within the Business Card artboard because you created them using the Artboard tool. If you want the guides to span all artboards and the pasteboard, create global guides using the Selection tool instead.

Prepare a photo for the business card

The design of the business card uses a photo that is emblematic of the outdoor Pluralist brand, but the busy visual nature of the photo would affect the readability of the type. You'll use Photoshop to blur the area of the photo where the type will go.

1 Switch to Adobe Bridge CC. In the Lesson01 folder, select the file Hiking_05_0347.NEF and press Enter/Return. This starts Adobe Photoshop CC, and because the photo is a raw file, Photoshop opens it in Adobe Camera Raw.

2   In Adobe Camera Raw, click Open Image to open the image in Photoshop.

It's a full-size raw file, so resizing it to the much smaller dimensions of the business card will speed processing. You can make it the same size and dimensions of the business card by using the Crop tool.

3   Select the Crop tool (![crop icon]) (C), and from the first pop-up menu in the Options bar choose W x H x Resolution. This setting lets you specify width, height, and resolution in pixels per inch.

4   In the three fields next to the pop-up menu you just changed, enter **3.75in**, **2.25in**, and **300**, respectively, and then press Enter/Return.

Those values correspond to the height, width, and resolution needed to completely cover the business card including its bleed size. Typing **in** after the value in the field specifies inches as the unit of measure, in case the document was set to another unit of measure. If you know the current unit of measure in the document, you don't need to add it on to the value in the dimension fields.

The crop rectangle is now shorter than the image height because the aspect ratio of the values you entered is different than that of the image. At this time you can recompose the image within the new aspect ratio before you commit to the crop, but there's no need to for this lesson.

5 Press Enter/Return to apply the current crop. The image will shrink onscreen because it was resampled to the lower pixel dimensions you specified, which still meets the resolution requirements for print.

6 Choose View > Fit in Window (Ctrl-0/Command-0).

7 Choose Filter > Blur > Tilt/Shift, and drag the center dot down to reposition the blur effect over the line of people so that they remain sharp.

8 Drag the upper dashed line down so that it's closer to the line of people but still high enough that the blur transition is gradual.

9 Drag the ring around the center dot until the blur strength is 45.

Although Tilt/Shift blur is normally intended to simulate the narrow depth-of-field effect of a tilt-shift lens, it comes in handy here as a way to apply a blur along a straight line.

10 Click OK to close the Blur Gallery.

11 Choose File > Save As and make sure you save the file as **Hiking_05_0347.tif** in the Lesson01 folder. For Format, choose TIFF; make sure Embed Color Profile is selected, and click Save. If the TIFF Options dialog box appears, for Image Compression select ZIP, and then click OK.

Note: If you get an alert after selecting ZIP, select Don't Show Again and click Yes.

12 Exit Photoshop.

Add elements to the business card

The business card will reuse the Pluralist logo and text from the stationery along with the photo you prepared. You'll add those now.

1 In Illustrator, with the Business Card artboard still selected, choose View > Fit in Window.

2 Choose File > Place, select the file **Hiking_05_0347.tif** in the Lesson01 folder, and click Place.

Tip: If you have trouble positioning the graphic in Step 3, make sure the View > Smart Guides command is deselected.

3 Position the loaded place icon at the top-left corner of the red lines marking the bleed area of the Business Card artboard, and click.

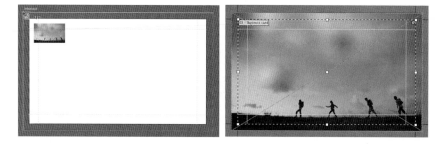

4 Choose Object > Arrange > Send to Back, and choose Select > Deselect.

5 Choose View > Fit All in Window.

6 Select the Selection tool (![icon](.)) (V), click to select the white Pluralist logo on the stationery, and Shift-click to select the logo's dark background pattern.

7 Alt-drag/Option-drag the selected logotype and its background to the business card, aligning them with the top-left corner of the red bleed guide. The Alt/Option key creates a copy as you drag.

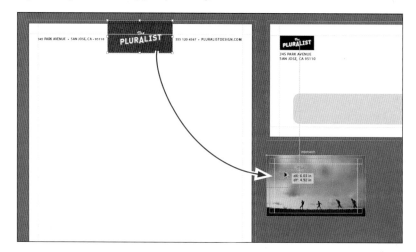

8 Choose Edit > Preferences > General (Windows) or Illustrator > Preferences > General (Mac). If Transform Pattern Tiles is selected, deselect it. Click OK to close the Preferences dialog box.

9 Zoom in, switch to the Selection tool, and drag the right edge of the background to the left until it's about halfway across the business card.

A green vertical Smart Guide should appear when you've dragged the edge to the center of the artboard. Note that if you have trouble doing this, make sure you specifically drag the edge of the logo background, not the middle and not any corner handle.

You used the Direct Selection tool to drag just the edge of the background rectangle because if you used the Selection tool to drag the right edge, the pattern would become distorted.

10 Use the Selection tool to reposition and resize the logo within its background rectangle. Make sure you're composing within the artboard edge (the printable area marked by the black page border) and not including the bleed area (marked by the red outline).

11 With the Selection tool, Alt-drag/Option-drag to copy the address text from the envelope to the business card, positioning it to the right of the Pluralist logotype and background.

12 With the text frame still selected, drag the bottom-right handle down to make room for two more lines of text.

13 Double-click the phone number text near the top-right corner of the stationery, and select the phone number.

14 Select the Type tool ([T]) (T), click the business card at the end of the address text, press Enter/Return, and choose Edit > Paste.

15 Repeat steps 11 and 12 to copy the website address and add it to the end of the contact information on the business card.

16 With a text insertion point still in the business card contact info text, choose Select > Select All, and in the Control panel set the Font style to Bold and the size to 8 pt.

17 If needed, use the Selection tool to adjust the sides of the contact info bounding box so that no text lines are broken.

18 With the text frame still selected, click the white color swatch in the Control panel.

19 With the text frame still selected, in the Appearance panel (Window > Appearance) choose Stylize > Drop Shadow from the fx menu at the bottom of the panel.

20 In the Drop Shadow dialog box, select Preview and enter **0.01** for the X Offset, Y Offset, and Blur. Click OK. The slight drop shadow helps set off the text from the background image.

21 Choose Edit > Deselect, and choose View > Guides > Hide Guides.

22 Choose View > Fit All in Window.

Congratulations! You've completed a set of visual identity materials by adding a business card to a stationery and envelope design.

23 Save the document, and then close it.

Next you'll apply similar elements to a mockup of a package.

Mocking up a package design in Illustrator

When you want to use linear perspective to create depth in Illustrator CC, it takes no time at all to set up a perspective grid. You can then forget about the technical points of perspective drawing and simply concentrate on your artwork. In this example you'll use the Perspective Grid to add a logo and illustration to a box mockup.

1   In Illustrator, choose File > New, choose the Print profile, click the portrait (tall) Orientation button, and click OK.

2   Select the Perspective Grid tool ( ) (Shift-P). The perspective grid appears.

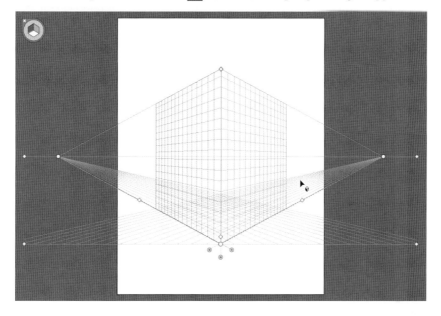

3   Try dragging the various Perspective Grid controls:

  • The diamond-shaped handles at the bottom left and bottom right move the entire grid.

  • The diamond-shaped handles at the top-left and top-right sides control the height of the horizon line.

  • The circular handles on the left and right sides of the grid change the angles of each plane.

4 Choose View > Perspective Grid > One-Point Perspective > [1P-Normal View] to see a preset for one-point perspective. Then choose View > Perspective Grid > Three-Point Perspective > [3P-Normal View] to see a preset for three-point perspective.

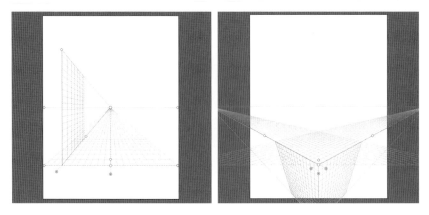

Now that you've seen how the Perspective Grid works, you can use it to draw in perspective as you mock up a package design in the next section.

5 Close the current untitled document window without saving changes.

6 In your Lesson01 folder, double-click the file package_start.ait.

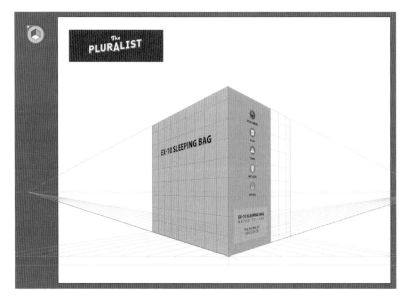

This file contains a box that was drawn using the Perspective Grid. Next you'll add a logo and a photo to it.

7 Choose File > Save As, and make sure you save the file as **package.ai** in the Lesson01 folder.

Adding the logo to the package

The logo is already present in the document. You'll add it to the package mockup in perspective.

1 With the Selection tool, drag a selection rectangle around the logo and its background.

2 Select the Perspective Selection tool () (Shift-V), and click the left plane of the cube in the plane switching widget.

3 Alt-drag/Option-drag the selected logo objects to the box. Because you selected the left plane and dragged with the Perspective Selection tool, the objects attach to the left plane of the Perspective Grid.

4 Position the logo at the top of the box so that it is centered.

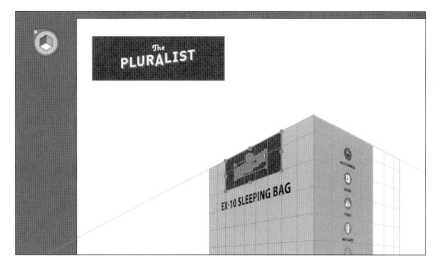

5 Choose Select > Deselect.

Adding the photo to the package

Now you're ready to add the photo to the box in perspective.

1 Arrange the Adobe Bridge and Illustrator document windows so that you can see both the Lesson01 folder in Adobe Bridge and the package document in Illustrator at the same time.

2 In Adobe Bridge, locate the sleepingbag.tif file, and drag it into the Illustrator document.

3 Zoom out until you can see the entire sleeping bag.

4 Using the Selection tool, Alt-Shift-drag/Option-Shift-drag a corner handle toward the center of the image to scale down the sleeping bag until it's about the same height as the box.

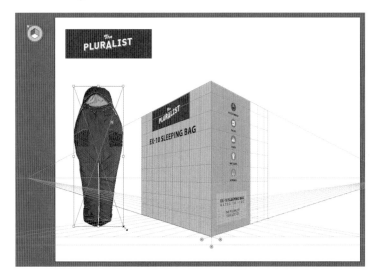

Bitmap vs. vector graphics

Pixel- or raster-based applications, such as Photoshop, are unbeatable when it comes to producing photographic or continuous-tone images. However, these images are composed of a fixed number of pixels, resulting in a jagged—or pixelated—look when they are enlarged. The following illustration clearly shows the difference between a resolution-independent vector graphic (left) and a resolution-dependent pixel-based graphic (right).

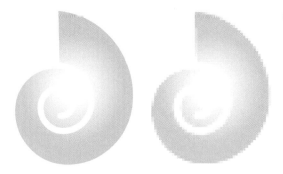

With Illustrator, you create vector graphics—artwork that is made up of points, lines, and curves that are expressed as mathematical vectors. Vector-based graphics are resolution independent; they can be scaled to any size without losing quality or crispness. You can also use the Image Trace feature to convert bitmap graphics to vector graphics, which is useful for creating expressive effects, recoloring images using Live Paint, or simplifying an image.

When you use the Selection tool, holding down Shift scales proportionally and holding down Alt/Option scales from the center.

One of the restrictions of a Perspective Grid is that a bitmap image, such as a photo, can't be used on it. Fortunately, the Image Trace feature can produce a faithful vector version of the image that can be used in the perspective mockup. The image is rather large, though, so the tracing will go much faster if it's downsampled.

5 With the sleeping bag image selected, choose Object > Rasterize. Leave the settings at their default except for Resolution; choose Medium (150 ppi) and then click OK. For this mockup, 150 ppi is sufficient and will trace much faster than 300 ppi.

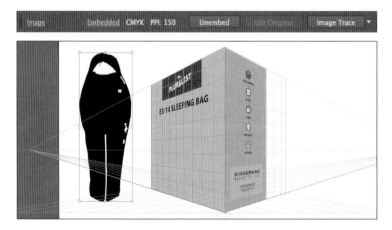

6 With the sleeping bag image still selected, click Image Trace in the Control panel.

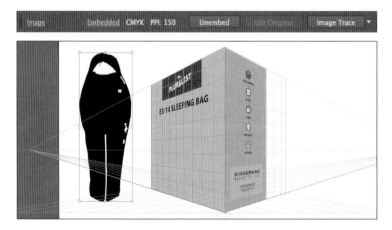

By default, Image Trace produces a black-and-white image, but you can change the tracing results. You'll use a preset instead of having to adjust individual settings manually.

7 In the Control panel, choose High Fidelity Photo from the Preset pop-up menu. The resulting trace may take a few moments depending on your computer.

About Image Trace

Many great design ideas start out as great pencil sketches on paper. To keep the precious spontaneity of such hand-drawn scribbles, it's best to bring the graphics straight into Illustrator and trace them. Placing a scanned file into Illustrator and automatically tracing the artwork with the Image Trace command is the easiest way to do so. The following illustrations show (from left to right) magnified views of original image pixels, Image Trace results with the Black and White preset, and Image Trace results with the High Fidelity Photo preset.

Image Trace automatically converts placed images into detailed vector graphics that are easy to edit, resize, and manipulate without pixelation. And, as Illustrator fans know already, Image Trace enables you to produce stunning-looking illustrations by changing rasterized images into vector-based artwork. You'll appreciate how quickly you can re-create a scanned drawing onscreen, maintaining its quality and authentic feel.

The pixels of the original image, first traced as black-and-white line art, are now traced as color line art. The original image pixels are still retained, but hidden, in case you want to change the tracing settings again. Now that the result looks much like the original photo, you can make the tracing results permanent by expanding them.

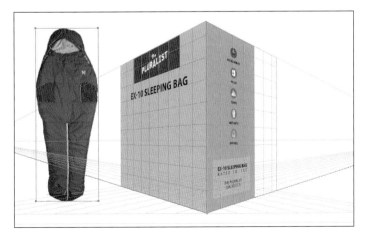

8 In the Control panel, click Expand. The tracing results are now permanently converted into Illustrator paths, so you'll see a large number of path handles when it's selected.

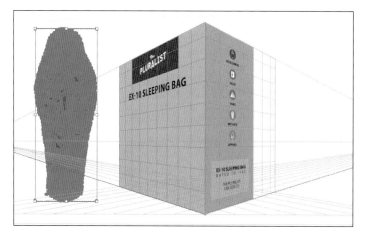

9 Select the Rectangle tool ( ) (M) and in the plane switching widget, click in the area outside the cube to deselect all planes because you don't want the next object to be in perspective.

10 With the Rectangle tool, Shift-drag a square around the top of the sleeping bag. If it contains a fill pattern, press the D key to reset its colors to the default black stroke and white fill.

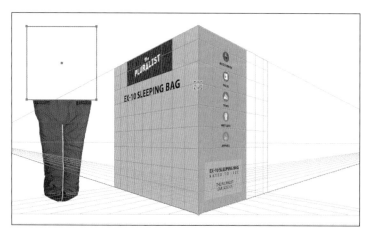

11 With the Selection tool, click the rectangle and Shift-click the sleeping bag.

12 Choose Object > Clipping Mask > Make. The rectangle now crops the sleeping bag.

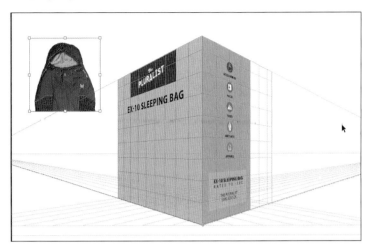

13 With the clipping mask still selected, in the Control panel click the link icon between the W and H fields to lock proportions, and then in the W field, enter **3.5 in**.

Note: If you can't find the W and H fields in the Control panel, the display may be too narrow. You can change the same fields in the Window > Transform panel instead.

14 With the Perspective Selection tool, click the left plane in the plane switching widget, and drag the sleeping bag image to the box.

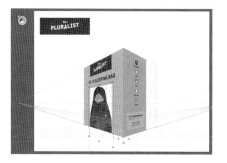

You'll notice that the area outside the sleeping bag is opaque white. Fortunately, because the graphic is now a vector tracing there is a quick way to make the white area transparent.

15 With the Selection tool, double-click the sleeping bag image on the box. The rest of the document dims, indicating that you have entered isolation mode for the sleeping bag object.

The gray bar across the top of the window also indicates isolation mode and displays how deeply the isolated objects are nested.

16 Double-click again, repeating if necessary until the path representing the white area is selected.

17 In the Color panel (Window > Color), click the Fill proxy, and then click the None swatch.

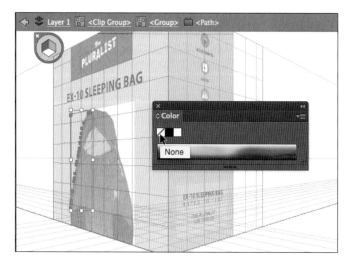

18 Press Esc to exit isolation mode and return to editing the entire document. You may have to press Esc more than once; you'll know you've finally exited isolation mode when the gray bar disappears.

19 Repeat steps 16 through 18 to remove the white fill from the other side of the area around the sleeping bag.

20 Choose View > Perspective Grid > Hide Grid.

Congratulations! You've applied consistent branding to a package mockup using the Illustrator Perspective Grid, and earlier to a stationery set.

21 Save the document, and then close it.

Creating a background image for social media

Social media websites are increasingly visual in nature, and more of them give you the opportunity to personalize or brand your profile page with large images. Creative Cloud tools make this not only easy, but flexible. Having a flexible document will save you time, because the layouts of social media sites constantly change; as more sites emerge and you extend your branded presence to them, those new sites have different layouts than the ones you already use.

The layers feature in Creative Cloud software, such as Photoshop CC and Illustrator CC, lets you maintain social media branding images as components you can rearrange as needed to keep up with the latest changes in social media website layouts, not just for desktop and laptop computers, but for mobile devices as well.

A background image must stay out of the way of foreground content, and that makes it more challenging to create than a simple cover image. Pay attention not only to where the page content normally appears, but how it moves as a browser window is resized and where it appears on mobile versions of the site. On some services, such as Twitter, the content is centered, which frees up the sides, giving you an opportunity to have a background photo and use the sides for important graphics, such as your logo. In this section you'll create a large background image with a side bar on the left.

1   Switch to Adobe Bridge CC. In the Lesson01 folder, select the file BeachCamp. jpg and press Enter/Return. This opens the file in Adobe Photoshop CC.

2   Choose File > Save As, choose TIFF from the Format menu, and save the file as **social-background.tif** in the Lesson01 folder, using the same TIFF settings as the other TIFF documents you've saved in this lesson.

3   In the Layers panel (Window > Layers), double-click the Background layer, name it **Beach**, and click OK. In Photoshop, a Background layer is opaque and at the bottom of the Layers panel so you can't add layers under it. Converting the image to a non-Background layer lets you position a solid color layer under it. The solid color layer will stand in for the background color you can set on sites such as Twitter.

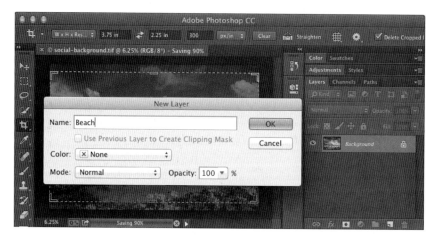

4   In the Layers panel, Alt-click/Option-click the Create New Fill or Adjustment Layer button ( ) and choose Solid Color; for Name enter **Background Color** and click OK. Pressing the Alt/Option key is what gave you the opportunity to name the layer as you created it, although you can also rename it at anytime.

5 In the # (Web hexadecimal color) field, enter **85b2c7** and click OK.

6 In the Layers panel, drag the Background Color layer below the Beach layer.

7 Press C to select the Crop tool, and in the Options bar choose Ratio from the first pop-up menu.

8 Drag the top-left corner of the crop rectangle down and to the right until the lower third, horizontal overlay line crosses the heads of the two people sitting on the beach on the left, and so there's roughly equal space on either side of those two people. Press Enter/Return until the crop rectangle disappears.

9 In the Layers panel, select the Beach layer and click the Add Layer Mask button (▢) at the bottom of the Layers panel.

10 Select the Gradient tool () (G), and in the Options bar, click the gradient picker, and then click the first gradient preset, which is named Foreground to Background because that gradient starts with the foreground color and ends with the background color.

11 Press the D key to reset the foreground and background colors to their default, a white foreground and black background.

12 In the Layers panel, click the mask for the Beach layer to select it.

13 Shift-drag the Gradient tool from left to right starting about halfway between the right edge and the person in the red jacket, and ending at the right edge. This fades out the Beach layer, revealing the background.

14 With the Gradient tool still selected, in the Options bar, click the gradient picker, and then click the second gradient preset, which is named Foreground to Transparent because that gradient starts with the foreground color and ends with transparency. This will be useful because you want to add to the existing gradient in the mask, not replace it.

15 Press the X key to exchange the foreground and background colors, and then Shift-drag the Gradient tool vertically from just above the bottom edge and up about the same distance as the first gradient you applied to the mask.

Right now this image is very large. You'll set its pixel dimensions to a more typical display size.

16 Choose Image > Image Size; change the unit of measure to Pixels; enter a Width of **1440** and leave Height alone; make sure Resample is selected and Bicubic Sharper is chosen in the Resample menu; and click OK.

17 Choose View > Fit on Screen.

> **Tip:** If you want to experiment with different background colors, simply double-click the Background Color layer.

This simulates how the background would fade out to this background color when displayed full screen on a 1440-pixel-wide display. On a smaller display the fade will be less visible or not visible at all, but on a larger display the image will clearly not reach across the screen.

Simulating page content

Now you'll create a placeholder for where Twitter content would appear over the background.

1 Select the Rectangle tool (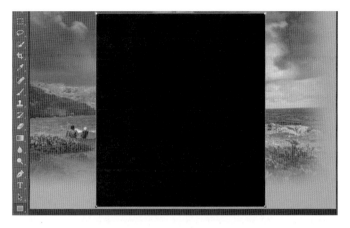) (not the Rectangular Marquee tool), make sure Shape is selected in the first menu in the Options bar, and drag a rectangle in the middle of the canvas.

2 In the Options bar, set the Fill color to white and the Stroke color to none, enter **865** for W and **900** for H.

3 In the Options bar, choose Align to Canvas from the Path Alignment icon menu, choose Horizontal Centers from the same menu, and then choose Top Edges from the same menu. This centers the shape across the canvas and aligns it to the top.

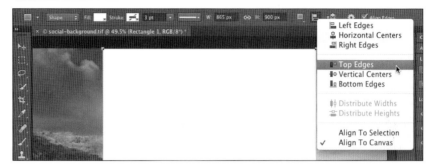

4 Press Enter/Return, and then press the 3 key to set the Opacity of the layer to 30%. Now you can visualize how the background distributes itself across a 1440-pixel-wide display with Twitter content in the middle.

5 In the Layers panel, double-click the Rectangle 1 layer, rename it **Content Placeholder**, and then press Enter/Return.

Adding a logo to the side bar

Because the background will be pinned to the top-left corner of a web browser window, that's the best corner for key branding information, such as a logo and tagline.

Note: If the measurement readout is not in pixels, right-click/Control-click a ruler and choose Pixels. If the rulers are not visible, choose View > Rulers.

1   Choose File > Place, select the Pluralist_logo.ai file in the Lesson01 folder, and click Place. In the Place PDF dialog box, simply click OK.

2   Drag the logo file to align it with the top-left corner of the canvas.

3   Shift-drag the bottom-right corner of the logo file until the measurement readout shows that it's 240 pixels wide; then release the mouse and press Enter/Return.

The alignment with the center content may appear to be a little loose, but keep in mind that the center content will shift to the left on smaller web browser windows. The idea is to find a good compromise that works across a range of browser window widths.

Adding text to the side bar

Now you'll add the tagline to the side bar.

1   Select the Horizontal Type tool (⬚) (T) and drag a text frame below the logo that ends near the top of the hill.

2   Type the text **Outdoor Gear**, press Enter/Return, type the text **We're ready when you are**, and then press Ctrl-A/Command-A to select all of the text in the frame.

3   In the Options bar, choose Myriad Pro as the font and 22 pt for the size, click the Center Text icon, and click the color swatch to set the type color to white.

4   Highlight the text "Outdoor Gear," and in the Options bar set the style to Bold.

5   In the Options bar, click the Character/Paragraph panel toggle icon, and then click the All Caps icon.

6 Select the text "We're ready when you are," and if needed fit the entire phrase on one line by reducing the font size in the Options bar or in the Character panel.

7 Click the Paragraph panel tab to bring it forward. For Add Space Before Paragraph enter **10 pt** and press Enter/Return to apply the value. Then press Ctrl-Enter/Command-Return to apply the changes to the text and exit the text frame.

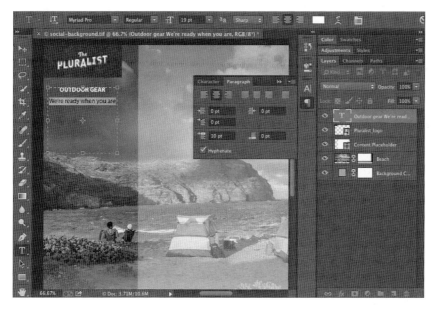

Moving image content seamlessly

It would be preferable if the two people sitting on the beach were centered under the logo, but they shifted to the right when the image was enlarged to fill a 1440 px display. Fortunately, you can instantly and seamlessly reposition the two people using the Content-Aware Move tool.

1 Select the Beach layer thumbnail (not its mask).

2 Select the Lasso tool (![lasso icon]) (L) and drag a selection marquee around the two people. It does not have to be precise.

3 Select the Content-Aware Move tool (), and turn off Sample All Layers in the Options bar.

4 Drag the two people until they're centered under the logo. The Content-Aware Move tool automatically adjusts the transition between the selection and background, and also removes the person on the right of the pair so that a duplicate is not left behind.

5 Choose Select > Deselect. Now there is more visual continuity from the top to the bottom of the side bar.

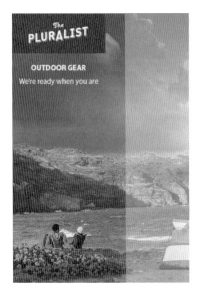

Exporting the final version

If you don't need to make any more changes, you can export this background for the web.

1 In the Layers panel, hide the Content Placeholder layer, because it should not be part of the exported background.

2 Choose File > Save for Web.

3 In the Save for Web dialog box, choose a JPEG preset that achieves the best balance between image quality and file size, because a larger image file size will slow down display of the profile page. Try starting with the JPEG Medium preset.

▶ **Tip:** Click the 2-Up or 4-Up tab to compare the original to different optimization settings.

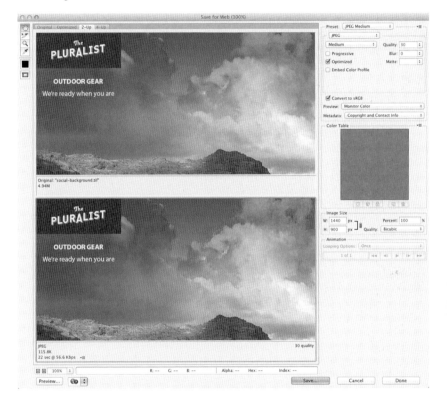

4 Make sure Convert to sRGB is selected, and click Save.

5 Save the file as **social-background.jpg** in the Lesson01 folder.

6 Save the document, and then close it.

Tip: If you know that the social media website accepts PNG images, you can also hide the Background Color layer so that the image fades to transparency instead of a solid color. The advantage of this is that you won't have to export the image again if you change the background color on the website.

7   Switch to Adobe Bridge, select the social-background.jpg file you just exported, and drag it into a web browser window to see how it looks. It appears on a white background because it requires a web page background color that's the same as the background color you used in Photoshop to fade out the image.

8   Close the web browser window.

Note that the settings used for the Twitter background in this lesson were based on the specifications at the time this book was written; always check your social media sites for current information on image sizing and page composition. Keep in mind that different websites highlight different areas of their background or cover images. On some websites the center of the image is the most important region, and on others it's the top. And remember to test background and cover images on a range of display sizes, including mobile devices. Typically, viewers will see less of a large image on smaller devices, and on some small devices it may not be displayed at all if the website designers decide not to allocate space for it on the layout.

Wrapping up

You've learned many of the Creative Cloud features that are important for preparing assets for projects. Throughout this book, you'll see how the assets you worked on in this lesson fit into larger workflows.

Review questions

1 How can you speed up the process of finding files and folders in Adobe Bridge?

2 Why would you use Adobe Bridge to synchronize your color settings when you're working within Adobe Creative Cloud applications?

3 What are some practical uses for artboards?

4 What two steps are required before you can drag an object to a specific perspective plane?

5 How is the Content-Aware Move tool useful in Photoshop CC?

Review answers

1 Select a file or folder and choose File > Add to Favorites. The file or folder will appear in the Favorites panel in the left panel group of the Adobe Bridge window where you have easy access to it. Alternatively, you can drag the file or folder—or even an application—directly into the Favorites panel.

2 Adobe Bridge provides centralized access to your project files and enables you to synchronize color settings across all color-managed Creative Cloud applications. This synchronization ensures that colors look the same in all Adobe Creative Cloud components. If color settings are not synchronized, a warning message appears at the top of the Color Settings dialog box in each application. It is highly recommended that you synchronize color settings before starting to work with new or existing documents.

3 You can use artboards to organize related components of a project in a single Illustrator file, such as an envelope, business card, and letterhead; maintain multiple pages of an interactive online project; or store multiple versions of a project.

4 You must select the Perspective Selection tool and select a plane on the perspective plane widget.

5 The Content-Aware Move tool saves time because it automatically fills in deleted objects by matching the lighting, tone, texture, and noise of surrounding areas instead of requiring you to manually patch the area.

2 CREATING A PRINT LAYOUT

Lesson overview

In this lesson you'll learn the skills and techniques you need to put together a sophisticated print magazine:

- Using Mini Bridge and Adobe Bridge CC to preview and select files

- Creating a document in InDesign CC

- Removing a background in Photoshop CC

- Working with layer comps in Photoshop CC files

- Adjusting raw images

- Importing and styling text

- Laying out graphics efficiently

- Working with transparency

You'll probably need between one and two hours to complete this lesson. Download the project files for this lesson from the Lesson & Update Files tab on your Account page at www.peachpit.com and store them on your computer in a convenient location, as described in the "Getting Started" section of this book. Your Accounts page is also where you'll find any updates to the chapters or to the lesson files. Look on the Lesson & Update Files tab to access the most current content.

Quickly identify and import files using Adobe Bridge CC and Mini Bridge. Add text and graphics in a variety of file formats and take advantage of advanced layout tools in Adobe InDesign CC. Then prepare your document for high-quality printed output.

Note: If you have not already downloaded the project files for this lesson to your computer from your Account page, make sure you do so now. See "Getting Started" at the beginning of the book.

Setting up

If you've ever looked at a folder full of files and were unsure about which one you should open, you may want to consider taking advantage of Adobe Bridge CC. Using Adobe Bridge to find the right document is often easier than using the standard Open dialog box, because Adobe Bridge gives you tools to inspect documents without opening them. Adobe Bridge can preview many file types produced in Adobe Creative Cloud. For InDesign CC files, Adobe Bridge can display the fonts and links in an InDesign document, and you can preview the document's pages.

You'll use Adobe Bridge to locate a partially completed InDesign document that you'll use for the exercises in this lesson. The document represents the latest issue of a printed magazine.

1   Start Adobe Bridge, and make sure the Essentials workspace is selected at the top of the Adobe Bridge window.

2   Navigate to the Lesson02 folder on your hard drive. Within that folder, select, but don't open, the file Magazine_Start.indt.

3   In the Preview panel, click the arrow buttons under the document preview to see the other page in the InDesign document. Using Adobe Bridge to page through InDesign documents without opening them can save you a lot of time.

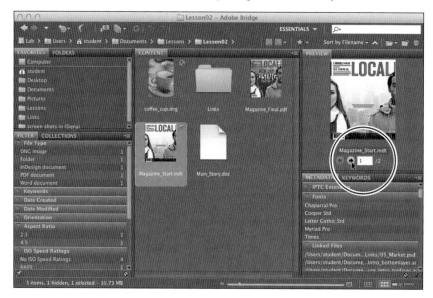

Tip: If the thumbnails in Adobe Bridge are hard to see, drag the slider at the bottom of the window to enlarge them, or press Ctrl-+/ Command-+.

4   Notice the chain-link badge at the top-right corner of the selected InDesign document icon in the Content panel. This badge indicates that you can inspect the links in the InDesign document. You'll do that next.

5   Scroll the Metadata panel until you find the Linked Files pane, where you can view a list of the files linked to this InDesign document. Click the disclosure triangle to reveal the list.

Above the Linked Files pane is the Fonts pane, where you can see which fonts are used in the InDesign document.

6   Select the file Magazine_Start.indt, and then choose File > Open With > Adobe InDesign CC (default).

Magazine_Start.indt is a template—it opens as a new, untitled document (see the sidebar "Jump-starting design and production using templates"). You'll save this document under a new name; the template file will remain unchanged so that you can always go back to it if you need to start over.

7   In InDesign, choose File > Save. In the Save As dialog box, navigate to the Lesson02 folder, name the document Magazine.indd, choose InDesign CC document from the Save As Type/Format menu, and then click Save.

Tip: You can customize the visibility of menu items in InDesign. Selecting a predefined workspace may result in some menu items being hidden. If you can't find the menu item you're looking for, choose Show All Menu Items at the bottom of the menu (if available), and choose Reset Workspace from the same menu.

Navigating through the document

Before making any changes to the document, navigate through its pages so you can plan which elements you want to customize.

1   Choose Window > Workspace > Advanced to lay out all the panels you'll need for this lesson and make all menu commands visible.

2   Use the navigation buttons in the lower-left corner of your document window to navigate through the pages of the magazine. Then use the menu next to the current page number to return to the first page.

You'll notice that the magazine contains alternate covers, one on page 1 and another on pages 2 and 3. The second cover includes a fold-out flap on the right, which is why it's a two-page cover.

3   Click the Pages button in the right panel dock to open the Pages panel.

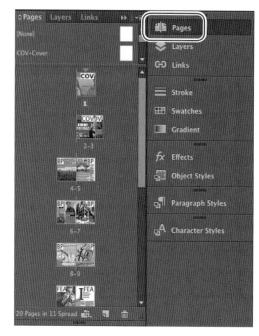

Jump-starting design and production using templates

When you produce a certain type of document repeatedly, such as a monthly issue of a magazine, you can save time by starting each issue from a template. A template is an InDesign document that contains any custom design elements and production settings you save into it, such as master page layouts, background elements, placeholder frames for text and graphics, and text and object styles. When you open a template, it opens as a new, untitled InDesign document. Using templates as the basis for frequently created documents is faster and easier than opening an old version and deleting all the content.

To create your own template from any InDesign document, choose File > Save As, and then choose InDesign CC Template from the Format menu. Template documents use the .indt filename extension.

If necessary, enlarge the Pages panel by dragging its lower-right corner downward so you can see preview images of all pages. Double-clicking a page in the Pages panel will open that page in the main document window. Double-clicking the page number under the preview image will center the page spread in the main document window.

4 Click the Pages button in the right panel dock again to close the Pages panel.

Viewing the reference document

In the Lesson02 folder is a PDF version of the completed magazine that you can use as a reference as you work through this lesson. This time we'll use Mini Bridge, a version of Adobe Bridge that you can use as a panel inside InDesign for easier access to the assets you want to bring into an InDesign document.

1 In InDesign, choose Window > Mini Bridge. If you see a Launch Bridge button, click it now.

2 Navigate to the Lesson02 folder and double-click the file Magazine_Final.pdf. The PDF file should open in Adobe Acrobat Pro.

3 In Acrobat choose View > Page Display > Two Page View and View > Zoom > Fit Width. Then use the arrow keys on your keyboard to navigate through the spreads.

You'll notice that the first cover does not match the InDesign document you opened. The reason is that the Photoshop CC file containing the two people has a background that needs to be removed. You'll do that soon.

4 When you're done, return to InDesign. You can leave the PDF document open for reference.

Removing a background in Photoshop

Extracting a subject from a background is one of the most time-consuming tasks a designer faces. The most difficult part of this task is precisely masking out the edge, especially where hair or fur is involved. The Truer Edge selection technology in Photoshop CC offers excellent edge detection and masking results in less time.

1 In InDesign, use Mini Bridge to navigate to the Links folder inside your Lesson02 folder and double-click the file Cover_Models.psd to open it. In the Layers panel, select the Original layer.

2 Choose Select > Load Selection, select model selection from the Channel menu, and then click OK.

3 Choose any selection tool (such as the Rectangular Marquee tool), and then click Refine Edge in the Options bar.

Note: The Refine Edge button is available in the Options bar only when both a selection and a selection tool are active. When only a selection is active, you can still open Refine Edge by choosing Select > Refine Edge (Control-Alt-R/Command-Option-R).

4 Click the View icon and choose On Black from the drop-down menu to make the changes easier to see. Then click the View icon to close the drop-down menu.

5 Set the Radius slider to 30 px. Increasing the Radius makes Refine Edge extend its evaluation area farther out from the original selection edge, which allows more of the woman's hair to be included. However, it also creates unwanted semitransparent areas in parts of the woman's jacket and man's jacket.

You may find it easier to observe these changes if you zoom in; remember that Photoshop View menu commands and magnification keyboard shortcuts still work while a dialog is open.

6   Turn on Smart Radius. When Smart Radius is on, notice how the selection is automatically looser by the woman's fine hair and tighter along the edge of the man's jacket. Applying Smart Radius lets you apply a larger Radius that accommodates softer areas by automatically tightening the Radius on sharper transitions along the same selection edge.

Tip: If you aren't sure if Smart Radius should be on, toggle the option and observe its effect on both the soft and hard transitions along the selection edge.

7 In the Refine Edge dialog box, select the Refine Radius tool (✑). Drag along the hair edge near the woman's shoulder to extend the radius outward to include more of her hair.

8 Press the L key, a shortcut for choosing the On Layers View Mode, so that you can evaluate how the current mask looks over the underlying layer. Press the B key to return to the On Black View Mode. Toggling back and forth can help you see more clearly whether the quality of the mask meets your standards.

Notice that there are some faint gray spots on the red sweater along the shoulder and arm. These are currently part of the mask, but those areas should not include any transparency. Although Smart Radius reduced these areas, it did not remove them entirely.

9 Alt-drag/Option-drag the Refine Radius tool over the shoulder of the woman's jacket near the edge to exclude that area from the Radius and restore maximum opacity. Alt-dragging/Option-dragging the Refine Radius tool is the same as choosing the Erase Refinements tool ( ), which is the opposite of the Refine Radius tool.

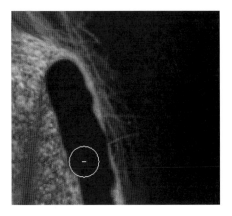

10 Select Decontaminate Colors to remove color fringing by replacing edge colors from the original background with colors from the new background so that the upper layer blends in more effectively. If the initial results don't seem optimal, you can adjust the Amount slider to achieve the most believable level of color fringe removal.

11 Choose New Layer with Layer Mask from the Output To menu, and then click OK.

12 In the Layers panel, notice the new layer Original Copy and its mask. Be sure to click the eye icon for the Cityscape layer to display it, and notice how the subject is now composited with the cityscape seamlessly, including individual hairs.

13 Choose File > Save As, navigate to Links folder inside the Lesson02 folder, name the document Cover_Models.psd, and click Save. If you're asked to replace the existing file, click Replace. In the Photoshop Format Options dialog box that appears, click OK without changing the settings. Then close the document.

Modifying an InDesign document

Now that you have created a document from the InDesign template, you can adjust it just as you can any other InDesign document. You can replace illustrations and photos, add and stylize text, and even change the document layout settings you've acquired from the template.

Updating a linked file

You just updated a Photoshop file linked to an InDesign document. Naturally, this will change the final output of that InDesign document, so InDesign can notify you when files you've imported have been edited. The Preflight and Links panels can alert you to issues with linked files so that you can resolve any problems prior to your deadline.

1 Switch to InDesign. You'll now see a red dot at the bottom of the window labeled "1 error." Double-click the error text to open the Preflight panel, which constantly checks your document.

2 Expand the LINKS heading to reveal details. InDesign indicates that the Cover_Models.psd Photoshop file you just edited is now marked as a Modified Link.

3 Expand the Info section at the bottom for advice on resolving the error. It prompts you to update the file link using the Links panel.

4 Click the Links tab (grouped with the Pages panel) to open the Links panel. A yellow triangle indicates that the Cover_Models.psd file is modified.

5 Select the Cover_Models.psd file and click the Update Link button. The layout updates with the edited image, the error alerts disappear in the Links and Preflight panels, and the preflight indicator is now green and reads "No Errors."

6 Close the Preflight panel.

Working with multiple page sizes

The magazine cover looks good, but to give it a little more interest, the client wants to extend the right side of the cover using a fold-out flap. You'll create this by adding a page to the cover to create a spread. In addition, the page you add to the spread will use a smaller, narrower page size.

1   In the Pages panel, double-click page 1, right-click/Control-click the page 1 thumbnail, choose Insert Pages, and in the dialog box that appears, click OK.

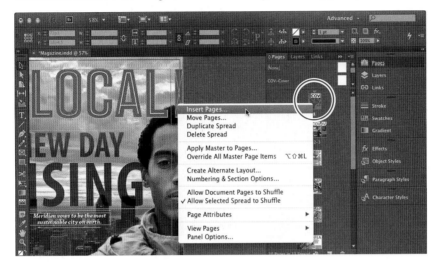

Because you created the new page from page 1, it's part of the page 1 spread.

2   In the Tools panel, click the Page tool ( ), and then click the new page you created. As you do this, the Control panel displays options for the selected page.

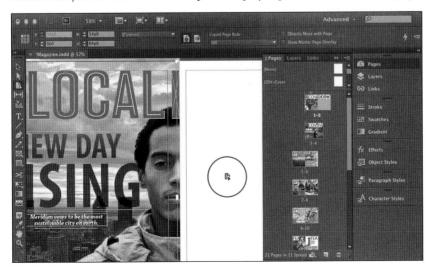

Tip: To adjust
the bleed and slug
areas, choose File >
Document Setup. If you
don't see the Bleed and
Slug options, click the
More Options button.

3 In the Control panel, change the page width (W) to 18p6.

4 In the Layers panel, click the disclosure triangles to the left of the Text layer and Background Art layer to reveal sublayers and the objects on those layers.

5 Click the square icon to the right of the <Cover_Models.psd> object label to select it.

6 In the Tools panel, click the Selection tool ( ). Drag the handle in the middle of the right edge to extend the graphic across the new page until the graphic is 93p1.6 wide, all the way to the right edge of the bleed area. The Control panel and the tool tip display the width as you drag.

7 Choose Edit > Deselect All.

You could have also selected the graphic by clicking it with the Selection tool, but on a busy layout like this one, using the Layers panel can be a more direct way of ensuring that you select exactly the object you want.

Selecting and editing frames that are stacked behind other frames

The sunrise image should also be extended across the new page, but you can't select it by clicking because it's completely behind the Cover_Models.psd image. Fortunately, there's more than one way to select it.

1 With the Selection tool, hold down the Ctrl/Command key and click the sunrise image. The first time you click, the bounding box for the Cover_Models.psd image may activate. Keep the Ctrl/Command key pressed and click again until the blue outline of the sunrise image activates. You can confirm this in the Layers panel by making sure the file Cover_Background.psd has a selected square to the right of it.

2 Once the sunrise image's frame is selected, you can drag the handle in the middle of the right edge until it is 74 picas wide. Of course, this works only when the image is larger than the frame that crops it in InDesign.

Tip: You can restack objects by dragging them up and down in the Layers panel.

Note: With multiple overlapping frames, you may need to Ctrl-click/Command-click repeatedly through the stack until the correct frame is selected.

3 Save your changes.

The second way to select the sunrise image would be to locate it in the Layers panel and click the square to the right of it, as you did with the Cover_Models.psd image.

Placing a Photoshop file with layer comps

Navigate to the last page, the back cover. Currently, the back cover is blank. You will first place the back page photo into the frame provided for it, and then make adjustments to the image in Photoshop.

1 Use the Selection tool to select the frame on the last page.

2 Choose File > Place. Navigate to the Links folder inside the Lesson02 folder. Select the file wifi_laptop.psd, select both Show Import Options and Replace Selected Item, and then click Open.

3 In the Image Import Options (wifi_laptop.psd) dialog box, make sure the Show Preview option is selected. In the Layers tab, notice that not all of the layers are turned on. Choose Sponsor On from the Layer Comp menu. This comp turns on the correct combination of layers, and the preview thumbnail updates to show the Local logo in the bottom-right corner. Click OK.

Because you enabled Replace Selected Item in the Place dialog box, the imported Photoshop file fills the frame you selected instead of being placed independently on the layout.

Tip: You can hide or show each layer independently. Layer comps are just a convenient way to hide or show preselected groups of layers.

4   To view the cover without page frames and guide lines, click and hold the Screen Mode button at the bottom of the Tools panel and choose Preview. When you're done previewing, choose Normal from the same menu. You can also toggle between Normal and Preview by pressing the W key.

The sunset would look better if it was a little more intense, so you'll now use Photoshop to alter the sky's color balance.

5   Make sure the frame containing the laptop image is selected, and choose Edit > Edit With > Adobe Photoshop CC (default).

6   In the Layers panel in Photoshop, click the disclosure triangle next to the Background layer group to reveal its contents. Select the Background Image layer at the bottom of the Layers panel.

7   In the Adjustments panel, click the Color Balance icon to add a new Color Balance adjustment layer immediately above the selected layer.

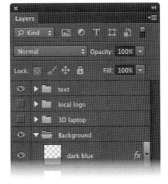

Tip: You can also do step 5 by choosing Edit > Edit Original, or by Alt-clicking/Option-clicking the image.

Tip: For a before and after comparison of the changes you made in the Color Balance panel while it's open, alternate holding down and releasing the Backslash key (\).

8 In the Color Balance panel, make sure Midtones is selected, and then enter **25** for the Cyan/Red slider, **0** for the Magenta/Green slider, and **−12** for the Red/Blue slider. Leave Preserve Luminosity selected.

Because the document now contains a layer that wasn't included in the original layer comps, you'll learn how to update the layer comps so they're properly preserved when you return to InDesign.

9 Open the Layer Comps panel (Window > Layer Comps). Two layer comps have already been defined, named Sponsor Off and Sponsor On. Click the box to the left of the Sponsor On layer name to enable that layer comp, and notice the effect it has on the visibility of the layers in the Layers panel and in the image.

A layer comp is simply a snapshot of the visibility, position, and layer style settings for various layers in the Layers panel. You may notice that the Color Balance layer you created was turned off when you turned on the Sponsor On layer comp. The reason is that that layer didn't exist when the layer comp was originally saved.

10 Turn on the Color Balance layer, make sure Sponsor On is highlighted in the Layer Comps panel (but don't turn it on), and then choose Update Layer Comp from the Layer Comps panel menu. Now the Sponsor On layer comp includes the Color Balance adjustment layer. Repeat this process for the Sponsor Off layer comp: Turn on the layer comp, turn on the Color Balance adjustment layer, and update the layer comp.

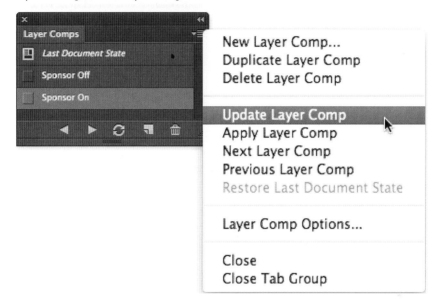

When you're placing a Photoshop file containing layer comps in InDesign, you can choose which version—or layer comp—you want to use in your publication without having to reopen and adjust the file in Photoshop.

11 Save changes, close the document, and then switch back to InDesign. Because the document was opened from within InDesign, InDesign is aware of the changes coming back, so no error appears this time.

> **Tip:** If you don't notice the difference made by the Photoshop edit, you can see a before and after comparison by choosing Edit > Undo and then Edit > Redo in InDesign CC.

12 With the back cover image still selected in InDesign, choose Object > Object Layer Options. If the Layer Comp menu shows Last Document State, choose Sponsor On, select the Preview check box to see the effect, and then click OK.

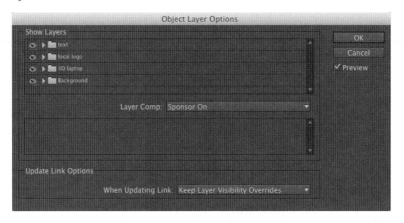

With the Preview check box on, you can choose different layer comps and see how each will look in the document before you click OK.

13 Choose File > Save.

14 Switch to Photoshop and exit Photoshop, and then switch back to InDesign.

Working with camera raw images

Note: Camera raw is not a single format. Each camera sensor model may have a different raw format and filename extension. Most camera raw formats can be converted to the DNG (Adobe Digital Negative) format, which is not proprietary to a specific camera manufacturer.

Camera raw format files are now common for high-quality digital photographs. The Camera Raw plug-in for Adobe Photoshop enables you to adjust a raw image and to then save it in a file format that you can place in InDesign.

1 In InDesign navigate to page 17. If it's not already selected, choose View > Screen Mode > Normal. If you don't see guidelines on the page, choose View > Grids & Guides > Show Guides.

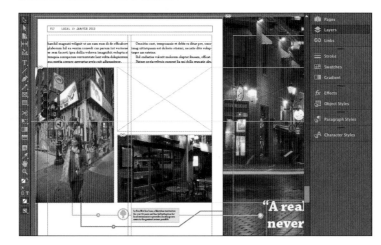

2 Select the empty graphics frame on page 17, and choose Object > Fitting > Frame Fitting Options. Select Auto-Fit, choose Fill Frame Proportionally, and click the center of the Align From proxy. These options ensure that no matter the size of the image, it will be sized to fit the frame and centered within it, saving you time in fitting the image to the frame.

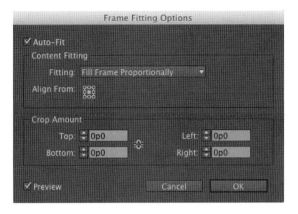

3 Click OK.

4 Switch to Adobe Bridge, and in the Lesson02 folder right-click/Control-click the file coffee_cup.dng and choose Open in Camera Raw from the context menu that appears.

▶ **Tip:** In step 4, you can also choose File > Open in Camera Raw or press Ctrl-R/ Command-R.

Notice that the image opens in the Camera Raw dialog box directly from Adobe Bridge. Although Camera Raw is a plug-in for Photoshop, Camera Raw can also be hosted by Adobe Bridge so that you don't have to open Photoshop just to run this plug-in.

Note: The reason you need to switch to Adobe Bridge is that Mini Bridge displays only the file formats its host program can import directly, and InDesign can't import DNG files.

5 To adjust the white balance in a camera raw image, you can choose from a predefined setting or pick a reference area within the image. Explore the different settings in the White Balance menu in the Basic panel and note the effect on the image colors. To adjust the color relative to an area in the image that should be a neutral mid-gray, select the White Balance tool (✐) from the Tools panel and then click inside the reference area. Clicking the White Balance tool on the coffee cup neutralizes the image colors. However, this photo is intended to convey a warm coffee-shop atmosphere, so restore the original white balance by choosing As Shot from the White Balance menu.

6 The image is a little flat, so it could use more contrast. To have Camera Raw determine a starting point for correction, click the underlined Auto text. From this point you can refine the automatic correction by dragging the sliders. The image is a little dark now, so increase the Exposure value to about 0.15.

7 Set Contrast to +35 by dragging the slider or entering the value.

8 Set Clarity to +20 by dragging the slider or entering the value.

Contrast is the overall contrast of the image, adjusting all levels equally. Clarity adjusts primarily midtone contrast, which enhances edges and helps images "pop."

Now you'll highlight the foam and coffee by using the Radial filter, which is a great way to apply an off-center vignette.

▶ **Tip:** Clarity enhances texture, so adding it accentuates skin features. For male faces adding Clarity can add character, and for female faces lowering Clarity can soften skin features.

9 Select the Radial Filter tool () and set Exposure to +0.50. This sets Exposure for the filter, not for the overall image.

10 Position the mouse over the foam on the cup, and drag away to create an ellipse around the top of the cup.

If the area outside the circle became lighter, the reason is that the Radial filter was set to apply the Exposure increase to the outside of the ellipse by default. You'll make sure it applies to the inside so that you can highlight the cup more effectively against the background.

11 Make sure that the Effect option is set to Inside.

Now you'll crop the image in Camera Raw, again saving a trip to Photoshop.

12 To specify a fixed aspect ratio for the Crop tool, click and hold the Crop tool button in the toolbar, and then choose an aspect ratio from the menu. We chose 4 to 5 to approximate the proportions of the frame in the InDesign layout, with a little room to spare.

13 Using the Crop tool, drag across the image to create a horizontal crop rectangle, as shown in the illustration.

At this point you could click Open Image to open the image in Photoshop and make further adjustments if necessary. That isn't needed for this exercise, so you'll simply save the file in a format that can be used in InDesign.

14 Click the Save Image button in the lower-left corner of the Camera Raw dialog box. In the Save Options dialog box, choose Save in New Location from the Destination menu, and select the Links folder inside the Lesson02 folder as the destination for the saved file. Type _cropped to add it to the document name, select Photoshop for the file format, and then click Save.

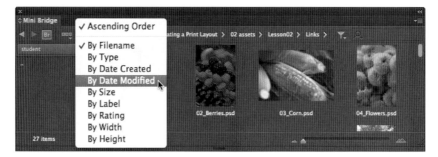

15 Click Done to close the Camera Raw dialog box and return to Adobe Bridge, and then switch to InDesign.

16 In InDesign use Mini Bridge to navigate to the Links folder inside the Lesson02 folder.

17 Click the Sort icon, choose By Date Modified, and deselect Ascending Order. This brings the coffee cup image to the top of the list because it's the most recent file you modified.

18 Drag the file coffee_cup_cropped.psd and drop it into the empty frame on page 17. The coffee cup image is automatically sized and centered in the frame because of the Auto-Fit settings you applied in step 2.

19 Move the mouse over the coffee cup image you just placed. Notice the Content Grabber in the middle of the image. Drag this indicator to move the image within the frame. The Content Grabber lets you adjust the position of the image within the frame without having to select a separate tool.

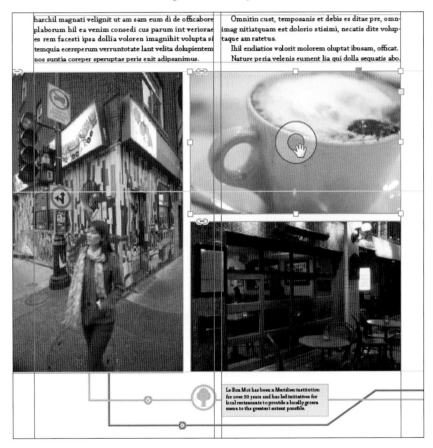

20 Save your changes.

Importing and styling text

You can enter text directly into an InDesign document by typing into the text frames. However, for longer text passages it is more common to import text from an external text document. You can style the text as part of the import process or manually change the text appearance later.

1   In InDesign navigate to page 12 of the magazine document.

    The text columns of the feature story are filled with placeholder text. You'll replace the placeholder text with text from a Word document.

2   Select the Type tool in the Tools panel, and click the cursor anywhere in the text in the two main text columns on page 12. Choose Edit > Select All. The text in both columns is selected because the text columns are linked. These text frames are also linked with the text frames on the next few pages.

3 Choose File > Place. In the Place dialog box navigate to the Lesson02 folder, select the file Main_Story.doc, select both Show Import Options and Replace Selected Item, and click Open.

4 Under Formatting in the Microsoft Word Import Options (Main_Story.doc) dialog box, select Preserve Styles And Formatting From Text And Tables and Customize Style Import. Click the Style Mapping button.

The Style Mapping dialog box enables you to match type styles defined in the Word document to type styles defined in the InDesign document. If you set up the styles with identical names, InDesign can perform the mapping automatically.

In this case, the Style Mapping dialog box shows that the Microsoft Word style Sidebar Bullet List doesn't match up with any style names in InDesign, so you'll have to map this style manually.

5 In the InDesign Style column in the Style Mapping dialog box, click [New Paragraph Style] to the right of the Microsoft Word style Sidebar Bullet List, and choose Sidebar Bulleted List. This maps the Word style to the InDesign style, which in this case is correct because the two styles are actually the same but were named slightly differently in the two programs.

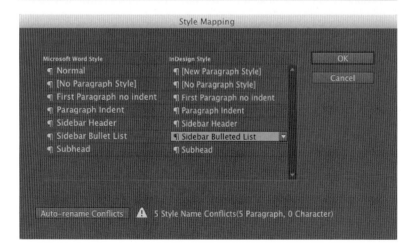

6 Click OK to close the Style Mapping dialog box, and then click OK to close the Import Options dialog box.

The imported text replaces the text in the two text frames and in the threaded text frames in the pages that follow, and the styles in the text take on the formatting defined by the same style names in InDesign. The text on page 12 overlaps the woman's arm; you'll fix that a little later.

7 Navigate to page 13 to see how the story continues through the threaded frames to the next spread.

Applying paragraph styles

In the story you just imported, one of the headings has the wrong style applied. It's body text, but it should be a heading. You'll fix this by applying the correct paragraph style.

1   While viewing page 13, open the Paragraph Styles panel (Window > Styles > Paragraph Styles).

2   Select the Type tool from the Tools panel, and click to place the flashing cursor inside the heading "Cobblestones, gentrification and local produce" almost two-thirds of the way down the second column. For a paragraph style, it is not necessary to select the entire paragraph.

3   In the Paragraph Styles panel, select the Subhead paragraph style. Notice the change in the text in the document window.

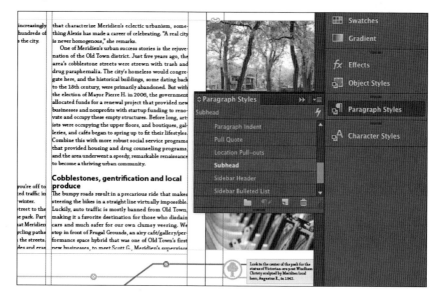

4   Save your changes.

Wrapping text around frames

Now that the text is formatted properly, it's time to fix the text overlapping the woman's arm on page 12.

1   With the Selection tool, click the woman's arm.

Although it's not currently visible, this image contains a clipping path that was drawn in Adobe Photoshop to cut the image out of its red background. You can also use this path as a text wrap boundary.

2   In the Text Wrap panel (Window > Text Wrap), click the third button from the left in the top row. This button wraps text around the shape of the object.

3   In the Text Wrap panel, choose Photoshop Path from the Contour Options: Type menu. There is only one clipping path stored in the document, Path 1, which appears in the Path menu. The clipping path is now used as the outline that Text Wrap follows when wrapping text around the image.

4   Make sure that the first text offset field is set to 0p9 (nine points). This specifies how far to keep the text away from the path.

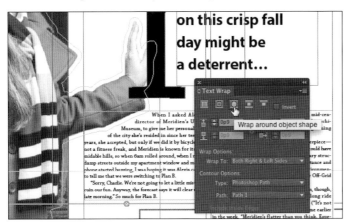

If you wanted to edit the shape of the object frame, you could select the Direct Selection tool to move the points on the clipping path.

Splitting paragraphs within columns and spanning paragraphs across columns

Some additional layout work needs to be done on page 13. To improve the composition of the page, you'll change the two columns on the page to three columns, and you'll convert some of the text into a sidebar. Fortunately, this task will be as simple as selecting text and choosing options in the Control panel.

1 Go to page 13, and with the Selection tool, click the two-column text frame.

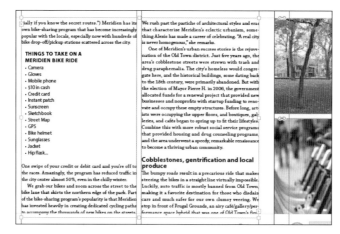

2 Choose Object > Text Frame Options, change the Number of columns to 3, and click OK.

3 With the Type tool, select the bullet list in the first column. Don't include the heading.

4 Make sure the Control panel is in Paragraph Formatting mode (the paragraph symbol is selected at the left edge), and choose Split 2 from the Span Columns menu in the Control panel.

5 Click the Type tool in the "Cobblestones, gentrification…" heading and choose Span 3 from the same Span Columns menu in the Control panel.

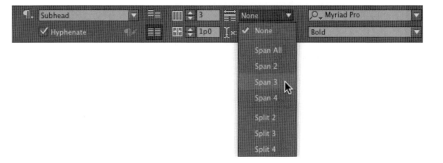

6 In the Layers panel, if necessary click the disclosure triangle next to the Text layer to expand it. Then click in the eye column for the Blue Box object to make it visible behind the sidebar. The box was added by the designer to accommodate the sidebar.

7 Save your changes.

Laying out multiple photos in a grid

You can quickly and easily lay out many photos at once for publications such as catalogs and yearbooks. InDesign simplifies and accelerates this process by letting you place multiple photos into a grid that you create as you import the images

1 In Mini Bridge, navigate to the Links folder. Select the files 01_Fruitstand.psd, 02_Berries.psd, 03_Corn.psd, and 04_Flowers.psd, and drag all four selected items to page 15 of the InDesign layout.

► **Tip:** The four files used in the exercise are easiest to select together if the sort icon in Mini Bridge is set to sort by filename, because the numbers in the filenames are sequential.

2 Position the loaded Place cursor at the intersection of the left margin and the cyan guide below the text frame on page 15. Begin dragging, and while the mouse button is still down, press the right arrow key once and then the up arrow once to create a 2 x 2 grid. Continue dragging to the bottom-right corner of the page to the intersection of the lower ruler guide and the right margin guide, and then release the mouse. Leave the images selected.

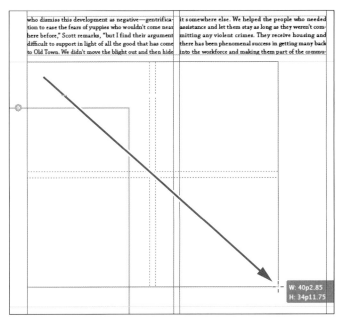

The images are set to fit within their frames, but you want these images to fill their frames while maintaining their proportions.

3 Choose Object > Fitting > Frame Fitting Options. In the dialog box, make sure the Preview check box is selected, select Fill Frame Proportionally in the Fitting menu, select the Auto-Fit option, and then select the center point in the Align From proxy. Click OK.

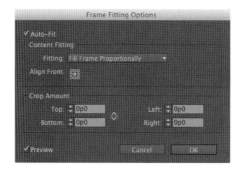

4 Choose Edit > Deselect All.

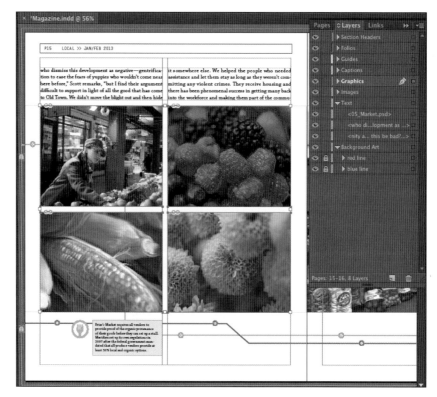

You've just imported and precisely fit four images into four frames in much less time than it would take to place them individually.

Creating live captions

Keywords, captions, and other metadata are becoming increasingly critical to print and online publishing. One way you can use metadata to enhance your publishing workflow is to automatically generate captions next to photos on the layout.

1   Choose Object > Captions > Caption Setup.

2   In the Caption Setup dialog box, set the first Metadata menu to Description. The other items in the menu are all forms of metadata that can potentially be included in an image by entering it using an application such as Adobe Bridge or as image metadata added by a camera.

3   If you see a second Metadata Caption line, click the minus sign at the end of the line to remove it.

4   In the Position and Style section, set the Offset to 1p0 (one pica, zero points), choose Captions from the Paragraph Style menu, and then choose Captions from the Layer menu. Click OK.

5   Use the Selection tool to select the image of the market on page 16. Zoom in to the bottom-left corner of the market image.

6   Choose Object > Captions > Generate Live Caption, and watch a caption appear to the specifications you set up in the Caption Setup dialog box.

This is a live caption because if the image description is changed (for example, using the Metadata panel in Adobe Bridge or Photoshop) when the image is updated in InDesign, the caption will update automatically. A live caption aligns with the left edge of the selected image by default; in this case that puts the caption in the gutter. You'll move the caption's left edge so that it will be readable in the bound magazine.

7 With the Selection tool, select the caption's text frame and drag the bottom-left handle of the text frame horizontally so that it snaps to the page margin. If the text disappears, drag the handle down a little farther to make the frame taller.

8 Press Ctrl-Shift-A/Command-Shift-A (the shortcut for the Edit > Deselect All command).

Shortcuts for editing objects

● **Note:** If the caption displays an error, such as <No intersecting link>, make sure the caption text frame touches the graphics text frame.

Repetitive layout tasks, such as aligning and distributing objects or customizing frame corners, are easy and quick in InDesign CC. You saw an example of this earlier when you used the Content Grabber to recompose an image inside a frame. You can take advantage of other layout tricks in InDesign CC.

1 Select the coffee cup image on page 17, and drag a corner of its frame to make the frame smaller. Notice that the image inside the frame resizes as well.

2 With the image still selected, deselect the Auto-Fit check box in the Control panel, and drag the corner of the image frame to enlarge it. This time the image doesn't scale with the frame. Choose Edit > Undo Resize Item, select Auto-Fit, and drag the corner to enlarge the frame back to its original size. Then deselect the image.

You control how Auto-Fit works in the same Frame Fitting Options dialog box you worked with earlier.

3 On page 15, hold down the Shift key as you click to select all of the four images you placed into a grid. Make sure Auto-Fit is selected in the Control panel.

4 In the Layers panel, click in the eye column to hide the Background Art layer.

5 Select the Gap tool in the Tools panel, and then position it in the gap between any two of the four images. You may want to zoom in so that the gaps are easier to see.

6 Click on the gap and drag with the Gap tool to control the space between the frames.

7 Shift-drag the Gap tool to adjust only the gap nearest the cursor. Each modifier key changes how the Gap tool works, so experiment with holding down the Alt/Option and Ctrl/Command keys as you drag the Gap tool.

Tip: To learn the shortcut keys, hold the cursor over various tools in the Tools panel until their tool tips appear; shortcut keys are listed in the tool tips.

Tip: When you release a spring-loaded tool that you're dragging, release the mouse button first and then the tool key.

Note: If you don't see the yellow handles, choose View > Extras > Show Live Corners. Also, make sure View > Screen Mode is set to Normal.

Now you'll use the Gap tool temporarily, using a feature called spring-loaded cursors. It's a quick way to use different tools with fewer trips to the Tools panel. Spring-loaded cursors take advantage of another time-saver: shortcut keys for tools. U is the shortcut key for the Gap tool.

8 Click the Selection tool in the Tools panel; it's the tool you'll typically use most of the time.

9 Position the Selection tool over a gap between images, and then press and hold the U key. Notice that the cursor changes to the Gap tool: Continue to hold down the U key as you drag to adjust the gap between the images. Release the mouse and then the U key; the cursor returns to the Selection tool.

Normally, pressing a shortcut key permanently switches tools. Spring-loading the cursor lets the new tool snap back to the old tool as soon as you release a shortcut key. Think of the difference this way: To use a shortcut key, briefly tap it; to use a shortcut key as a spring-loaded shortcut, hold it down until you're done.

10 With the Selection tool, click the image of berries, and then click the yellow control near the top-right corner of the image. The frame handles at the corners turn into diamond handles, which let you customize the shapes of the frame corners.

11 Drag any of the yellow diamond handles to adjust the corner radius of all corners. The corner radius value appears in the Corner Options section of the Control panel. Choose a corner shape from the Corner Shape menu below the radius value. Shift-drag a diamond handle to adjust just one corner, or Alt-click/ Option-click a diamond handle to change the corner shape.

▶ **Tip:** Alt-click/ Option-click the Corner Options icon (not the pop-up menu) in the Control panel to open the Corner Options dialog box.

▶ **Tip:** Another way to change corner shapes is to Alt-drag/Option-drag a corner handle.

12 In the Layers panel, click in the eye column for the Background Art layer to make that layer visible again.

Tracking text changes

Get to final copy faster by tracking text changes directly in your InDesign document. You can write, edit, and mark up text in InDesign CC without needing to import separate text files and remap styles every time there are copy changes.

1 Navigate to page 13. Choose Window > Editorial > Assignments, and then choose User from the Assignments panel menu. Enter a User Name, choose a Color, and click OK.

2   With the Type tool, click to place an insertion point inside the text story. Choose Window > Editorial > Track Changes. The top-left button in the Track Changes panel controls whether Track Changes is enabled, and the next button controls whether changes are visible. Make sure both buttons are on.

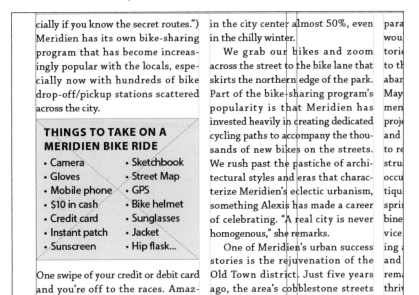

cially if you know the secret routes.") Meridien has its own bike-sharing program that has become increasingly popular with the locals, especially now with hundreds of bike drop-off/pickup stations scattered across the city.

THINGS TO TAKE ON A MERIDIEN BIKE RIDE

- Camera   • Sketchbook
- Gloves   • Street Map
- Mobile phone   • GPS
- $10 in cash   • Bike helmet
- Credit card   • Sunglasses
- Instant patch   • Jacket
- Sunscreen   • Hip flask...

One swipe of your credit or debit card and you're off to the races. Amazingly, the program has reduced traffic

in the city center almost 50%, even in the chilly winter.

We grab our bikes and zoom across the street to the bike lane that skirts the northern edge of the park. Part of the bike-sharing program's popularity is that Meridien has invested heavily in creating dedicated cycling paths to accompany the thousands of new bikes on the streets. We rush past the pastiche of architectural styles and eras that characterize Meridien's eclectic urbanism, something Alexis has made a career of celebrating. "A real city is never homogenous," she remarks.

One of Meridien's urban success stories is the rejuvenation of the Old Town district. Just five years ago, the area's cobblestone streets were strewn with trash and drug

para wou torio to th abar May men proje and to re stru occu tiqu spri bine vice ing and rem thri

Cobblestones, gentrification and local produce

The bumpy roads result in a precarious ride that makes steering the bikes in a straight line virtually impossible. Luckily, auto traffic is mostly banned from Old Town, mak-

our own clumsy veering. We stop in front of Frugal Grounds, an airy café/gallery/performance space hybrid that was one of Old Town's first new businesses, to meet Scott G., Meri-

styli a me and com spec

3 In the "Things to Take on a Meridien Bike Ride" sidebar, select the text 10 and type 25.

4 Choose Edit > Edit in Story Editor to open the Story Editor window and note the highlight color. Click in the highlighted text and notice that the Track Changes panel indicates that you are the user who edited the text.

If you see text highlighted in other colors, that's text edited by other users whom you can identify in the Track Changes panel.

cially if you know the secret routes.") Meridien has its own bike-sharing program that has become increasingly popular with the locals, especially now with hundreds of bike drop-off/pickup stations scattered across the city.

THINGS TO TAKE ON A MERIDIEN BIKE RIDE

- Camera
- Gloves
- Mobile phone
- $25 in cash
- Credit card
- Instant patch
- Sunscreen

- Sketchbook
- Street Map
- GPS
- Bike helmet
- Sunglasses
- Jacket
- Hip flask...

One swipe of your credit or debit card and you're off to the races. Amazingly, the program has reduced traffic in the city center almost 50%, even in the chilly winter.

We grab our bikes and zoom across the street to the bike lane that skirts the northern edge of the park. Part of the bike-sharing program's popularity is that Meridien has invested heavily in creating dedicated cycling paths to accompany the thousands of new bikes on the streets. We rush past the pastiche of architectural styles and eras that characterize Meridien's eclectic urbanism, something Alexis has made a career of celebrating. "A real city is never homogenous," she remarks.

One of Meridien's urban success stories is the rejuvenation of the Old Town district. Just five years ago, the area's cobblestone streets were strewn with trash and drug

paraphernalia. T would congregat torical buildings to the 18th cent abandoned. But Mayor Pierre H. i ment allocated f project that prov and nonprofits w to renovate and structures. Befor occupying the up tiques, galleries, spring up to fit t bine this with m vice programs tl ing and drug cou and the area un remarkable rena thriving urban co

Cobblestones, gentrification and local produce

The bumpy roads result in a precarious ride that makes steering the bikes in a straight line virtually impossible. Luckily, auto traffic is mostly banned from Old Town, making it a favorite destination for those our own clumsy veering. We stop in front of Frugal Grounds, an airy café/gallery/performance space hybrid that was one of Old Town's first new businesses, to meet Scott G., Meridien's supervisor of urban renewal.

stylishly dressed a medium-length and knit cap, th complemented b spectacles and a der bag.

5 Click inside the highlighted text you edited, and click the Accept Change button in the Track Changes panel.

6 When you're done, close the Story Editor window and the Track Changes panel.

7 Save your changes.

Preparing for printing

You've completed the design of the magazine. Because the document contains transparency effects, a few more adjustments are necessary to get the best print results.

Transparent areas in a document need to be flattened—or rasterized—when printed. For the best results, flattening should be done as the last possible step in your print workflow. Normally, it is performed by your print service provider. To keep transparency effects live until they need to be flattened, preserve the layers by saving your InDesign, Illustrator, and Photoshop files in their native formats.

You can help minimize the effects of flattening if you send your document output to devices that support the latest versions of PDF. To preserve transparency effects rather than flattening them when exporting a document as a PDF intended for printing, save your file in a format compatible with Adobe PDF 1.4 (Acrobat 5.0) or later by selecting the PDF/X-4 PDF export preset, for example. The Adobe PDF Print Engine (APPE)—widely embraced by OEM partners and print service providers since it was first released in 2006 and updated to version 2 in 2008—uses native rasterizing for PDF documents, ensuring file integrity from start to finish in a PDF-based design workflow. To learn more about the APPE, go to www.adobe.com/products/pdfprintengine.

Previewing how transparency will affect output

The Flattener Preview panel helps you identify which areas will be most affected by the flattening process. For this reason, the Flattener Preview panel is a useful tool that can help you determine if any areas of a document have transparency issues, so that you can resolve those issues before final output.

1 In InDesign navigate to page 8 of the magazine document.

2 To see which areas of your document are affected by transparency effects, open the Flattener Preview panel (Window > Output > Flattener Preview), choose Transparent Objects from the Highlight menu, and choose [High Resolution] from the Preset menu. In the Highlight menu, choose these commands in turn: All Affected Objects, Affected Graphics, and All Rasterized Regions. When you're done, choose Transparent Objects.

The areas affected by each Highlight option are highlighted in red, such as the text frame in the lower-right corner of the page. You can use the Effects panel to find out why that object is highlighted. Specifically, you're looking for a blend mode other than Normal in the menu at the top of the Effects panel, an Opacity lower than 100%, or an applied effect.

3 Using the Selection tool, click the text frame.

4 If the Effects panel is not visible, choose Window > Effects.

5 Double-click the group to select the frame inside the group. Now that the text frame is selected, the Effects panel reveals that the Fill uses the Multiply blend mode and is set to 85% Opacity. These are the options that create transparency in this object.

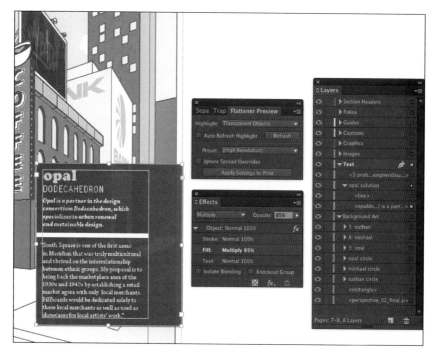

If the Flattener Preview panel reveals potential issues with how transparency will affect part of your document during output, you can decide what to do about those issues. For example, if you see that type or highly detailed vector graphics will become rasterized, you might decide to change the design to avoid the problem by moving critical objects so they don't overlap objects that use transparency or by avoiding the use of transparency in that area.

One thing to watch out for is text placed behind objects with transparency effects. Transparency affects all objects placed lower—or farther back—in the display stacking order. Printed text might not look as crisp as it should if it was converted to outlines and rasterized behind an object with a transparency effect. So, whenever possible, it's best to keep text in front of transparent objects in the layer order.

If you need to flatten your document as part of the export or print process, for the best results set the document's transparency blend space (Edit > Transparency Blend Space) to the color space (CMYK or RGB) of the target output device. For more information about working with transparency see "Best practices when creating transparency" in InDesign Help.

6   When you're done, in the Flattener Preview panel set the Highlight menu to None.

Checking the effective resolution of linked images

You can use the Links panel to verify that the linked images have a high enough resolution for your intended mode of output. The effective resolution of a placed image is defined by the resolution of the original image and the scale factor at which it is placed in InDesign. For example, an image with a 300 ppi (pixels per inch) resolution only has an effective resolution of 150 ppi when it's scaled to 200%.

For images to be viewed at screen resolution—published on a website or in a low-resolution PDF document, for example—an effective resolution of 72 ppi is sufficient. For general office printing, the effective resolution should be between 72 ppi and 150 ppi. For commercial printing, your images should have an effective resolution between 150 ppi and 300 ppi (or higher), depending on the requirements of your prepress service provider.

1 In InDesign open the Links panel. Choose Panel Options from the Links panel menu. In the Panel Options dialog box, in the Show column select the Actual PPI, Effective PPI, and Scale options. Click OK to close the Panel Options dialog box. If necessary, resize the Links panel so that you can see the additional columns.

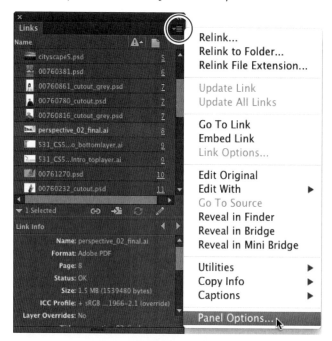

2   For each image placed in your document, check the actual resolution, the effective resolution, and the scale factor. For example, the cover image on page 1 has an actual resolution of 150 ppi but an effective resolution of 153 ppi because it was scaled by 98.2%. If a higher effective resolution is required for your print job, you could reduce the scale factor, which would show more of the image background; reduce the dimensions of the placed image, which is not really an option for the cover photo because it needs to cover the entire page; or select an image with a higher actual resolution—perhaps a close-up photo of the face rather than the wider shot that is used in this example.

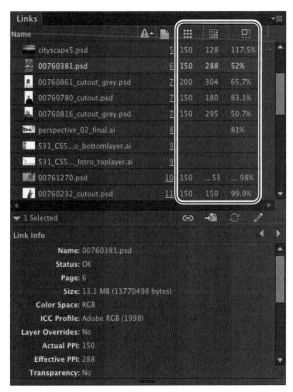

3   Close the Links panel.

Performing a preflight check

Rather than painstakingly checking through a list of possible problem areas each time you want to print or export a document, you can rely on InDesign to do all the work for you.

1   Click the preflight status indicator at the bottom of the document window and choose Preflight Panel. When the On check box is selected in the Preflight panel, InDesign continuously checks for possible problems while you're working on your document.

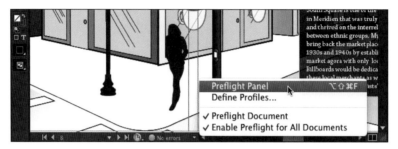

You can set up a preflight profile to specify which potential problems you want InDesign to look out for.

2   To define a preflight profile, choose Define Profiles from the Preflight panel options menu or from the same Preflight status menu you just used.

3   In the Preflight Profiles dialog box, click the New Preflight Profile button (＋) below the list of profiles to create a new profile. Name the new profile Resolution Check. Activate the Image Resolution option inside the IMAGES and OBJECTS category. Leave the Color Image Minimum Resolution set at 250 ppi, and then click OK.

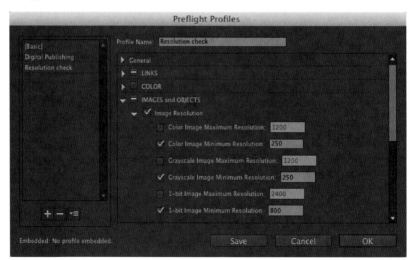

4   From the Profile menu in the Preflight panel, choose Resolution Check. If necessary, click the disclosure triangles next to the IMAGES and OBJECTS heading and the Info heading to expand their lists. InDesign finds several placed images that don't meet the set requirements. To review an error found by the Preflight check, click the page link in the Preflight panel. InDesign selects and jumps to the object causing the error. A description of the error and suggestions on how to fix the problem are provided in the Info section in the Preflight panel.

In this case, you would make judgments about which images in the error list have effective resolutions that are too low to be acceptable. You can then decide whether to reduce their dimensions on the layout so that their effective resolution increases, or you might go back to the source files for those images to see if they contain sufficient pixels to export higher-resolution versions that can replace the current versions.

5   Switch back to the previous preflight profile by choosing [Basic] from the Profile menu in the Preflight panel, and then close the Preflight panel.

6   Save your document.

Exporting to PDF

Exporting your document as a PDF file enables you to preserve the look and feel of your InDesign document in a device-independent format that can be viewed onscreen or printed on any printer. This can be particularly useful when you want to print a quick draft of your document on an inkjet printer at home or in your office. You can tweak the export settings, balancing quality and file size to create a PDF that is optimized to suit its intended purpose.

1 Choose File > Export. In the Export dialog box, navigate to the Lesson02 folder. From the Save As Type/Format menu, choose Adobe PDF Print; name the file Magazine_Print.pdf, and click Save.

2 In the Export Adobe PDF dialog box, choose [High Quality Print] from the Adobe PDF Preset menu. Review—but don't change—the settings for this export preset in the various panels of the dialog box, and then click Export.

3 Open the Lesson02 folder in Windows Explorer/the Finder. Right-click/Control-click the file Magazine_Print.pdf, and choose Open With > Adobe Acrobat Pro.

4 Use the page navigation controls in Acrobat to review the pages of the magazine. Pay special attention to the position and quality of the images you placed, the text styles you've adjusted, and the areas containing transparency effects.

5 When you're done reviewing, close the document in Acrobat and switch back to InDesign.

6 Close the InDesign document, and if you're asked if you want to save changes, click Save.

Review questions

1   How can you select a frame that is stacked behind another in an InDesign document?

2   How do you edit a page so that it's a different size than the rest of the document?

3   What is a layer comp?

4   What is the effective resolution of an image placed in InDesign?

5   What is the advantage of creating a preflight profile?

Review answers

1   To select a frame that is stacked behind another frame, hold down the Ctrl/Command key, and then click inside the frame you want to select. With multiple overlapping frames, you may need to click repeatedly until the correct frame is selected. You can also select the topmost frame, and then choose Object > Select > Next Object Below.

2   With the Page tool, select the page you want to modify, and then edit the page dimensions in the Control panel or by dragging the page handles.

3   A layer comp is a snapshot of the visibility settings of layers in a Photoshop document that can be used to organize multiple versions of a design in a single document. When placed in InDesign, you can quickly switch between the layer comps using the Object Layer Options dialog box.

4   The effective resolution of a placed image is defined by the actual resolution of the original image and the scale factor when placed in InDesign. For example, an image with a 300 ppi (pixels per inch) resolution has an effective resolution of only 150 ppi when scaled to 200%. Documents intended for print require images with a higher effective resolution than documents that will be viewed only onscreen.

5   A preflight profile represents the output requirements of a specific job. When you create your own preflight profile that's tailored to the requirements of your print service provider, InDesign can continuously check the state of the document and its assets, and alert you to any problems that may cause an issue at output time. Because problems at output time can be expensive to fix, catching problems early can save you time and money.

3 CREATING A MOBILE-FRIENDLY WEBSITE

Lesson overview

Adobe Creative Cloud includes Adobe Muse CC, which offers an easy way to use familiar Adobe design tools to create mobile-friendly websites for you or your clients without writing code. This lesson will introduce you to important skills and concepts:

- Planning the structure and design of your website

- Planning the website design

- Adding dynamic content, such as menus, a slide show, and parallax scrolling

- Adding a contact form

- Designing a mobile version of the site

- Previewing and testing your website

- Publishing your website

 You'll probably need between one and two hours to complete this lesson. Download the project files for this lesson from the Lesson & Update Files tab on your Account page at www.peachpit.com and store them on your computer in a convenient location, as described in the "Getting Started" section of this book. Your Accounts page is also where you'll find any updates to the chapters or to the lesson files. Look on the Lesson & Update Files tab to access the most current content.

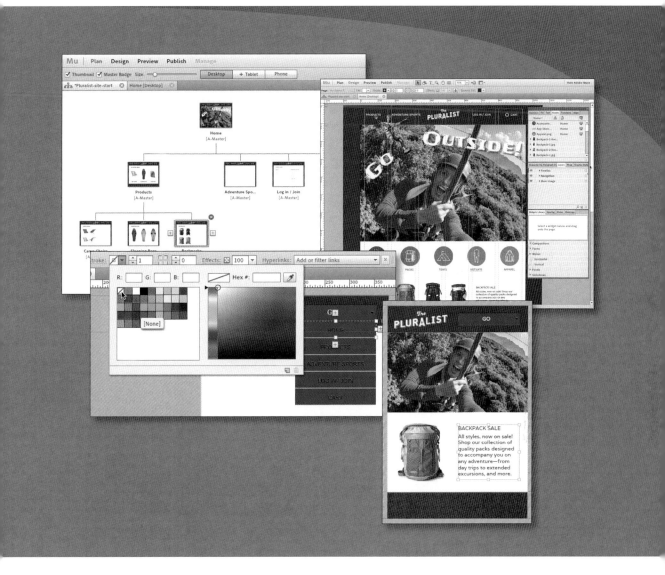

In this lesson, you'll use Adobe Muse to design and
publish a website that includes a layout for smartphones.

Note: If you have not already downloaded the project files for this lesson to your computer from your Account page, make sure you do so now. See "Getting Started" at the beginning of the book.

Designing a website with Adobe Muse CC

As a component of Adobe Creative Cloud, Adobe Muse CC sets itself apart from most website creation tools by letting you use familiar tools and commands, like those in InDesign CC and Photoshop CC. You can create your website by thinking like a designer, not a web programmer. This design freedom doesn't compromise the technical quality of the site because websites you create in Muse adhere to current web standards. Your sites can be mobile-friendly as well, because you can easily create a single site with layouts customized for desktop computers, tablets, and smartphones. When you create mobile versions of a website, they aren't just sized appropriately for the screen, but they also respond to touch gestures like swipes and pinches. These advantages help provide your site's visitors with a positive experience no matter how they view your site.

Adobe Creative Cloud also simplifies publishing and hosting of your Adobe Muse website by providing you with Adobe Business Catalyst web hosting services. Business Catalyst is available at multiple levels; as part of your Creative Cloud subscription you can host up to five live websites at the webBasics level of Business Catalyst or an unlimited number of trial sites. You can also upload an Adobe Muse site to another hosting service and publish it there. Either way you can use your own domain name for your website.

The ability to easily create websites with Muse and host them with Business Catalyst gives you a complete and familiar web design and publishing solution within Adobe Creative Cloud.

In this lesson, you'll be working in Adobe Muse CC.

Exploring an Adobe Muse project

When you design a website in Muse, the website pages are stored inside an Adobe Muse project file. Assets you use in the site, such as images, are stored outside the project file and are linked by reference, similar to how imported files are handled in other Adobe Creative Cloud applications, such as Adobe InDesign CC.

1 In Windows Explorer, Mac OS X Finder, or Adobe Bridge CC, navigate to your Lessons folder, open the Lesson03 folder, and then double-click the file Pluralist-site-start.muse. The file opens in Adobe Muse CC.

You first see the Plan view, which provides an overview of the pages in a site. From this view you can quickly lay out the structure of your website by adding and rearranging pages.

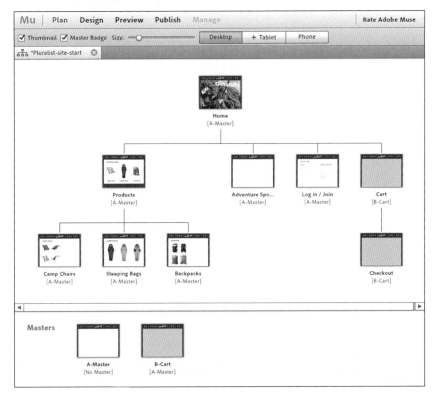

Tip: You can go to a page by double-clicking it in Plan view or by choosing Page > Go to Page (Control-J/ Command-J).

2 Double-click the Home page. It opens in its own tab in the Muse workspace. Page-editing tools appear at the top of the workspace, and panels appear along the right side of the workspace.

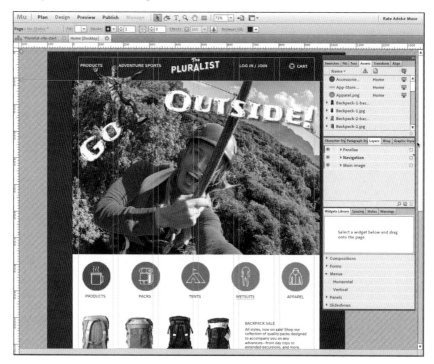

By clicking any of the five headings across the first row of the workspace, you can switch the view you see in the workspace:

- Plan displays the site map, which is where you started.

- Design displays an individual page, and it's the view you see now.

- Preview lets you interact with your website, simulating a web browser.

- Publish sends your website to the Adobe Business Catalyst web hosting service so that your website can go live on the Internet and become accessible to visitors if you make it public.

- Manage provides an administrative interface to your website after you've published it, so you can view visitor statistics, resource usage reports, and more.

3 Switch back to Plan view.

Below the five view headings are three buttons: Desktop, Tablet, and Phone. The site map you're currently viewing is for the Desktop version of the website. A plus (+) sign is located before the Tablet and Phone buttons because those versions of the site do not currently exist, but you'll add a Phone version later.

At the bottom of the workspace you see two master pages, which work similarly to the master pages in InDesign CC.

4 Without clicking, hover the mouse over various pages in the site map. Controls appear around each page as you move the mouse over them. These controls let you insert more web pages at the same level or at a lower level in the hierarchy. You can also drag pages to rearrange the website.

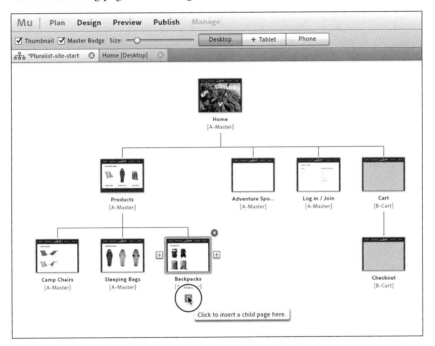

5 Double-click the Home page. It opens in its own tab in the Muse workspace, and switches to Design view.

6 Choose View > Fit Page in Window so you can see the entire page.

Blue horizontal guides span the workspace and end in handles near the vertical ruler on the left. These guides mark the header and footer areas.

7 Choose View > Hide Guides to see the design without the margin, column, and ruler guides. In Design view you can see and edit the design, but you can't preview interactivity, such as links. For that, you must be in Preview view.

▶ **Tip:** You can magnify or reduce the view using the Zoom tool or the View > Zoom In and View > Zoom Out commands.

8 Scroll down to and zoom in on the Backpack Sale text frame, and double-click it with the Selection tool. In the toolbar, notice that the Varela font is selected. Varela is a web font that can be automatically downloaded by the web browser viewing your site. Muse supports Adobe TypeKit web fonts so you can use a wide variety of high-quality fonts on your website. Access to TypeKit fonts is part of your Creative Cloud subscription.

Web fonts are discussed along with other font choices available to you in Chapter 4, "Using Fonts with Adobe Creative Cloud."

9 At the top of the workspace, click Preview.

10 Scroll down the page. You'll see some page elements animate as you scroll: The type moves off the sides of the page and the hanging zipline man slides off the screen to the right. There is also a slide show near the bottom of the page. You'll work with these features later.

11 Choose File > Preview Page in Browser. The web page opens in your default web browser so you can test it more effectively.

Adjusting a parallax scrolling effect

On the desktop Home page, scrolling the page controls an animation on the page. This effect is called *parallax scrolling*. You'll learn how to adjust this effect now.

For each object you can set a scroll point where motion changes (called a *key position*), and you can set the rate of motion relative to the scroll speed before or after that point. Although only vertical scroll position controls motion, you can set an object to move vertically or horizontally.

1 Switch to Preview view and scroll the page. Observe how the word Outside moves right until it's off the page.

Right now, three objects start moving when you start scrolling: The Go and Outside text, and the image of the zipline rider. Now you'll delay the start of the Outside text so that it doesn't begin moving until the zipline rider is close.

2 Switch to Design view and open the Home page.

3 With the Selection tool ( ), select the Outside text, click Effects in the toolbar, and then click the Scroll Motion button. The Scroll Motion check box is selected because the object already uses parallax scrolling.

4 Enter **148** for the Key Position. Notice that the T handle extending upward from the Outside text frame represents the key position.

5 For Motion Before Key, click the upward motion radio button and enter **1** as the vertical speed. Leave the horizontal speed setting at 0.

6 For Motion After Key, leave the vertical speed setting at 0. Click the rightward motion radio button and enter **1.5** as the horizontal speed.

▶ **Tip:** By applying different speeds to various objects, you can create a pseudo-3D motion effect. This simulation of motion parallax is where the term "parallax scrolling" originated.

When Key Position is set to 0, an object begins moving when the page begins scrolling. Increasing Key Position delays scrolling. Entering 1 for the upward Motion Before Key option ensures that the object will scroll up at the same speed that the page is scrolled until the key position is reached, and then it will begin moving horizontally at the Motion After Key speed.

▶ Tip: You can also apply parallax scrolling to page background or element background images.

7 Press Enter/Return to dismiss the Effects panel, and then preview the document in Muse or in a web browser.

Adding a mobile version of the website

With much of the desktop design complete, you can add a version of the website that's optimized for the small screen of a smartphone.

1 Switch back to Muse and switch to Plan view.

2 Click the + Phone button.

3 In the Add Phone Layout dialog box, choose Desktop from the Copy From menu. Make sure all three check boxes are selected, and click OK.

Muse duplicates the entire site map of the website but doesn't copy the objects because it's best to compose them specifically for the display size and proportions of a smartphone.

4 Double-click the A-Master page at the bottom of the window.

5 Choose View > Show Guides so you can see the header and footer guides.

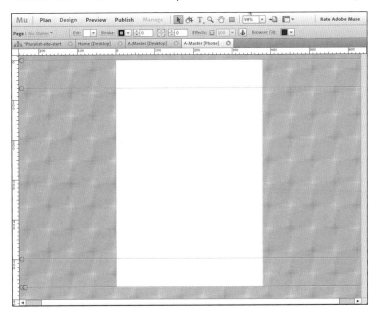

Now you'll create the phone version of the desktop master page, but you'll need to open the desktop version first.

6 At the top of the workspace, click the Plan view or the Pluralist-site-start tab to switch to the site map, and then click the Desktop button.

7 Double-click the A-Master page.

Notice that Muse distinguishes which layout an open document belongs to by appending [Desktop] and [Phone] to the page names in the tabs. The currently open page is A-Master [Desktop].

The desktop master page contains a white main page area, a dark blue header and footer, and a dark blue browser fill on the left and right sides. It also has menus at the top and bottom. The background elements will be easy to copy, but a phone screen isn't wide enough for the horizontal menu across the top, so you'll create a more compact phone version of the menu. But first you need to re-create the background elements of the master page.

8 With the Selection tool, click to select the rectangle across the top of the page, and choose Edit > Copy.

9 Click the A-Master [Phone] tab and choose Edit > Paste in Place. This command is often better than choosing Edit > Paste, which pastes an object in the middle of the screen.

10 With the Selection tool, drag the handles of the rectangle to resize it until it fits within the header area. As you drag a corner or side handle to a page edge or header guide, a red line appears and the handle snaps to the red line. When the sides of the rectangle align with the red lines on the left and right sides, it is set to 100% width so that it will always be as wide as the display. This helps adapt your design to varying display sizes.

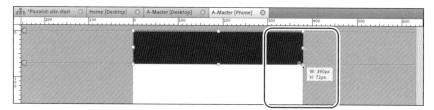

11 Return to the A-Master [Desktop] page and repeat steps 8 through 10 for the rectangle at the bottom that contains the pattern.

12 Return to the A-Master [Desktop] page and repeat steps 8 through 10 for the Pluralist logo.

Note: In Muse you don't have to Shift-drag corner handles to constrain an object to its original proportions. Muse preserves the original proportions when you simply drag a handle.

13 After pasting the Pluralist logo to the A-Master [Phone] page, use the Selection tool to drag the corner handles of the Pluralist logo to scale it down to about 75% of its original size.

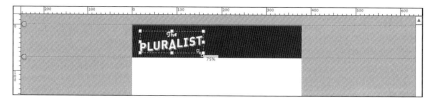

14 Click Preview to see how the page currently works. Try the different Preview Size options available in the toolbar.

15 Choose File > Save Site As, and save the file as **My-site.muse** in the Lesson03 folder.

Adding a compact menu for the phone layout

Adapting the website's top menu for a phone layout is quick because Adobe Muse provides easy-to-use widgets for commonly used objects, such as menus.

1   Switch to the A-Master [Desktop] tab. Note the four menu names across the top of the page: Products, Adventure Sports, Log In / Join, and Cart.

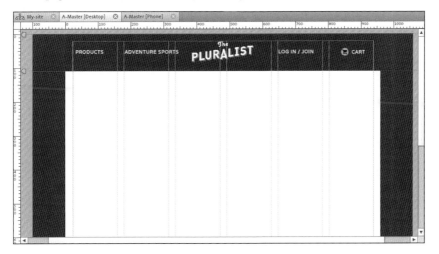

2   Switch to the A-Master [Phone] tab. In the Widgets Library, click to expand the Menus section and drag a Horizontal menu to the page. Resize it and position it so that it fits in the header to the right of the Pluralist logo. It should be about 32 pixels tall.

3 With the menu widget selected, in the Layers panel make sure the widget is on the Navigation layer. If it isn't, drag it to the Navigation layer.

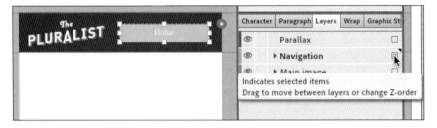

As in InDesign CC, Illustrator CC, and Photoshop CC, you can use the Layers panel to organize your document and more easily maintain the desired stacking order of page objects.

4 With the widget selected, click the white triangle at the top-right corner of the widget to reveal the widget options. Change the Menu Type to Manual and make sure the Direction is Horizontal.

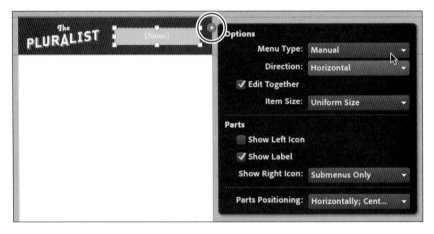

5 Double-click the menu (not the text) to reveal the controls for adding menu items, and click the one on the bottom with the hierarchical menu indicator. A new menu item appears below the existing menu item.

6 With the Selection tool, resize the new menu item so that its height and width matches its parent menu.

7 Click the submenu and then click to add another menu item below it; repeat until there are five items on the submenu.

8 With the Text tool (T) (T), edit the text of each menu item. Type **Go** for the first menu item, and name the rest of the menu items to match the top level menu on the desktop version of the Home page.

▶ **Tip:** If the submenu retracts into its parent menu, you can reveal it again by clicking the parent menu.

9 With the Selection tool, click the menu widget until the Fill control in the top toolbar displays the gray fill of the menu item. Click the Fill menu, choose the medium blue swatch near the right edge of the swatches, and set the Stroke menu to none.

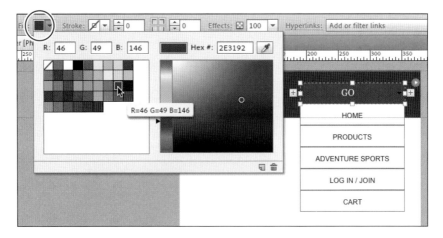

10 Click the menu item again to reveal the submenu, and click to select Home, the first individual submenu item. If the entire group is selected, click again, because you want to select only one of the submenu items.

Tip: When Edit Together is selected in a widget menu, editing one of the objects (such as changing the fill color) affects all of its siblings.

11 Apply the same Fill and Stroke colors you chose for the parent menu item.

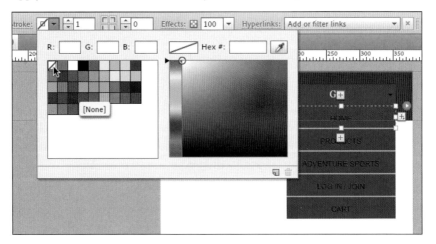

138 LESSON 3 Creating a Mobile-friendly Website

12 With the menu widget selected, click Menu in the Paragraph Styles panel (Window > Paragraph Styles) to format the text using a paragraph style. You may have to repeat this step for the submenu.

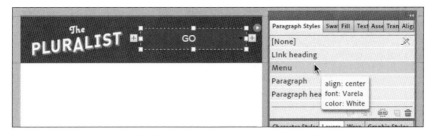

13 Click the Home menu item so that it is the only item selected and the Hyperlinks option appears in the toolbar. Click the Hyperlinks menu, and then choose Home in the Phone section.

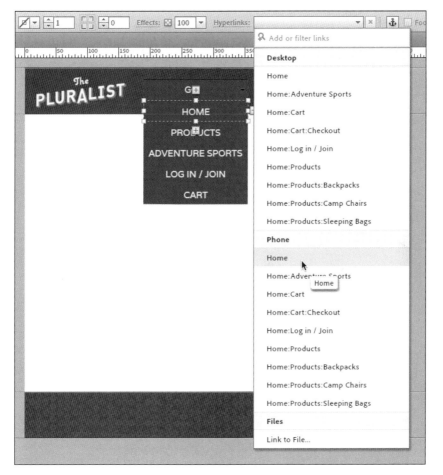

14 If the previous step caused the submenu to close, click the Home menu item to reveal it, and click Products until the Hyperlinks option appears in the toolbar. Click the Hyperlinks menu, and then choose Products in the Phone section.

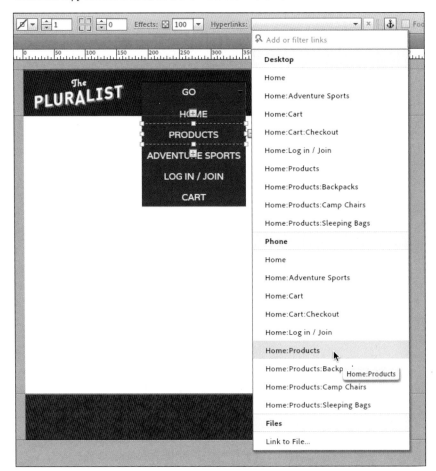

The Hyperlinks menu lists all pages in the site, so you don't have to type exact URLs for pages within the same site. You can use this technique to apply a hyperlink to other types of objects.

15 Repeat step 14 for the other three menu items.

16 Click Preview to test the menu.

17 Close the two A-Master tabs.

18 Save your work.

Adapting the main image

Next you'll copy the main image from the Home page, paste it into the Phone version of the Home page, and resize the image to fit.

1 Switch to the Home [Desktop] page, use the Selection tool to select the large image, and choose Edit > Copy.

2 Switch to Plan view. In the Phone version of the layout, double-click the Home page, and choose Edit > Paste.

3 With the Selection tool, resize the image so that it matches the full width of the phone display. As you did earlier, watch for the red lines to appear to confirm that the image aligns with the edges of the page.

4 With the Crop tool (![crop tool icon]) (C), drag the center handle on the top edge of the image to trim the image closer to the top of the woman's helmet so the image takes up less vertical space on the smaller phone display.

> **Tip:** If the expanded menu is in the way, go to A-Master [Phone] and click the menu to collapse it. Then return to the page you were working on.

5 With the Selection tool, reposition the image so its top edge meets the bottom of the header.

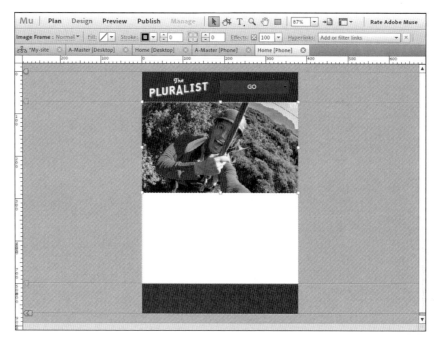

6 Switch to the Home [Desktop] page. For the phone layout you'll omit the row of icons below the main image. To save space, the icons will be a subsection under the Products menu item you added.

7 Select the orange backpack image, copy it to the clipboard, switch to the Home [Phone] page, and choose Edit > Paste. Position the image below the main image on the left side.

8 Copy and paste the Backpack Sale text frame from the Home [Desktop] page to the Home [Phone] page. Resize and reposition the text frame to the right of the backpack image.

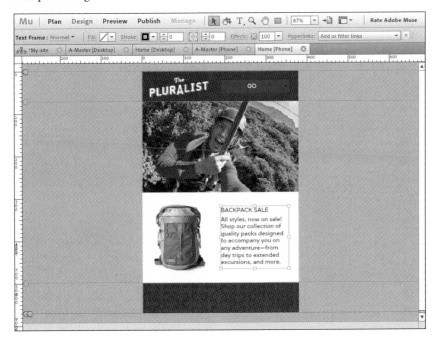

9 Scroll down to select the slide show widget (the image of the four hikers walking under clouds), and then copy and paste it from the Home [Desktop] page to the Home [Phone] page. Resize it to the full width of the phone display and position it below the Backpack Sale image and text. You may need to click the slide show more than once with the Selection tool to make the transformation handles appear.

As you reposition the slide show at the bottom of the page, notice that the footer automatically moves down to make room. Muse automatically adjusts the height of a page to accommodate content you add.

10 With the slide show widget selected, click the white triangle at the top-right corner of the widget to reveal the widget options. You can use these options to customize the slide show, but it isn't necessary to change any of the settings for this lesson.

11 Copy and paste the Outdoor Sports text from the Home [Desktop] page to the Home [Phone] page. You can maintain space between the last line of the text and the footer by extending the bottom edge of the text frame or by entering a value in the B (bottom) field in the Spacing panel (Window > Spacing).

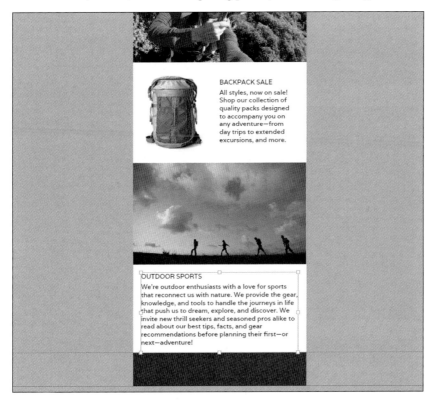

12 Click Preview to check your work. Notice that the bottom of the page appears to be cut off. The reason is that Preview displays only the Preview Size and orientation selected in the toolbar. The page is cut off exactly where it would be on the actual phone being previewed. To see the rest of the layout, scroll the display using a scroll wheel, scrolling trackpad, or the up arrow/down arrow keys.

13 Choose File > Preview Page in Browser. Notice that the browser preview does not restrict the height of the display; it's only restricted by the current size of your browser window. This is an important difference between previewing your site in Muse and in a browser.

14 Switch back to Muse and save your work.

When you publish your Muse site to Business Catalyst, the desktop, tablet, or phone layout is automatically delivered based on identifying information supplied by the viewer's device.

If you want more practice adapting layouts for mobile devices, you can add a Tablet layout and adapt the content of the site for that display size as well.

Adding a form

Muse comes with widgets for creating forms, so creating contact forms and membership registration forms is a snap.

In the site's Desktop version, the Log In/Join page is complete but is too large for a phone display, so you'll create a more compact version.

1 Go to the page Log In/Join [Phone].

2 In the Widget Library, expand the Panels section and drag an Accordion widget to the page from the Panels section.

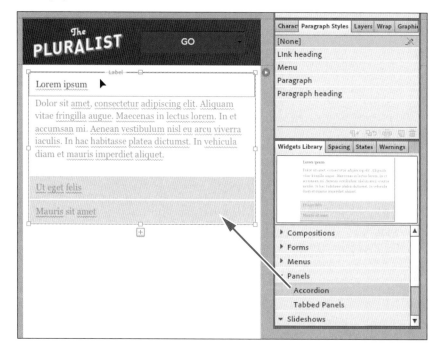

3 With the Selection tool, click the third accordion option until it becomes selected on its own, and press Delete. You'll need only two options in this accordion panel.

4 Resize the widget to fill the page with a small margin around it.

5 With the widget selected, click Paragraph in the Paragraph Styles panel to format the text.

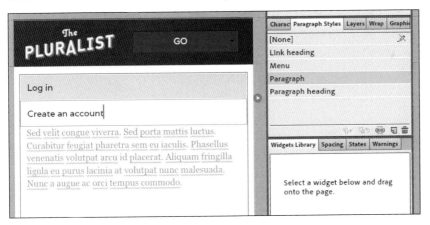

6 Double-click the first accordion heading and enter **Log in**.

7 Double-click the second accordion heading and enter **Create an account**.

8 Go to the page Log In/Join [Desktop].

9 With the Selection tool, click to select the form widget for the Log In section but don't include the heading.

10 Go to the Log In/Join [Phone] page, select all of the text inside the Log in section, press Delete, and then paste the widget you copied from the other page.

11 Repeat steps 9 and 10 to bring over the form widget for the Create an Account section.

Like the widgets you've seen before, when these form widgets are selected, they display the blue circle at the top-right corner that you can click to see the options provided by that widget. Form widgets let you add a wide variety of standard or custom fields. The Create an Account widget on this page uses a CAPTCHA image verification field to help deter automated spam programs from registering.

12 Preview the page in Muse or in a web browser. Click the accordion headings to test how they open and close.

13 Save your work.

Publishing your Muse website

The simplest way to publish your Muse website is to click Publish and use the Business Catalyst web hosting service that's included with your Creative Cloud subscription.

1 With your Muse website open, click Publish.

2 Enter a name for Muse to use to create the URL for your site, and click OK. Muse creates a URL with the name you entered, and opens it in your default web browser.

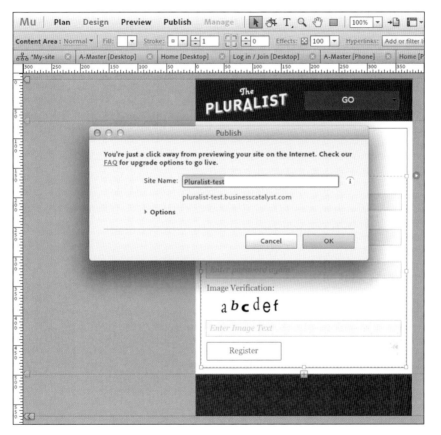

By default, the URL ends in businesscatalyst.com, but you can change the URL later. You can even use a custom domain name.

Note that at this point your site is not visible to search engines yet. However, it is visible to anyone who has the URL.

To modify the URL and other settings, and to launch the site, you need to manage it using the Business Catalyst website.

In-browser editing

Adobe Muse CC lets you assign areas of your website that authorized users can update from a web browser. You may want to enable this feature if you design a site for a client and want to let the client update specific areas of the website. In-browser editing can't be used to make changes to layout or structure, so you don't have to worry about the integrity of the website.

3 In Muse, click Manage to launch Business Catalyst in your web browser, opening an administrative page for your website.

4 Click each of the headings on the left to explore the settings and traffic reports that Business Catalyst provides for your website. The Site Settings section contains the options for managing the URL and domain names used by your website.

5 When you're done, close your web browser.

If you want to use another web host, you can use Muse to upload and update your website to that hosting service using FTP. When you must update your site, Muse can minimize update time by uploading just the modified files. To use FTP instead of Business Catalyst, choose File > Upload to FTP Host. You can also export a site as static HTML by choosing File > Export as HTML.

Wrapping up

You've learned how to design a standards-compliant website without writing code by using Adobe Muse. You also created a mobile version of a Muse website, created menus and forms, and were introduced to the parallax scrolling effect that's becoming increasingly popular on websites.

Review questions

1   What are the two ways to preview a Muse page or website before publishing it, and what is the difference between them?

2   In the parallax scrolling effect, what is the key position?

3   How do you ensure that an object always spans the entire width of a display?

4   What is the advantage of using widgets to add elements to a Muse web page?

5   What are the two ways to publish a Muse website?

Review answers

1   Muse can preview a site within the software with Preview view, or in a web browser using the Preview Page in Browser/Preview Site in Browser commands. The Preview view in Muse can restrict the preview of a Tablet or Phone layout to the size of those displays, whereas Preview Page in Browser/Preview Site in Browser commands always preview using the size of your web browser window.

2   For parallax scrolling, the key position is the vertical position on the page where motion changes. You use the scroll motion effect options to specify what motion happens before and after the key position.

3   As you drag a side or corner handle to resize an object, a red guide appears to indicate that releasing the mouse will snap that side of the object to the edge of the page. If you use the red guides to snap the left and right sides of the object to the left and right page edges, Muse will automatically specify the object width as 100% of the page width.

4   Widgets save you time because you can add full-featured page elements without writing code. You can add widget elements to a page by dragging and dropping, and you can set their options by pointing and clicking.

5   You can publish a Muse website to Adobe Business Catalyst web hosting, or you can export the website HTML and CSS code and upload it to your own web host.

4 USING FONTS WITH ADOBE CREATIVE CLOUD

Lesson overview

The way you set up your documents and create your assets will affect how easily and efficiently you can design your work. This lesson will introduce you to some important skills and concepts:

- Understanding which font formats are best for print and web projects

- How to choose appropriate font types in various Creative Cloud applications

- Using TypeKit fonts

You'll probably need less than one hour to complete this lesson. Download the project files for this lesson from the Lesson & Update Files tab on your Account page at www.peachpit.com and store them on your computer in a convenient location, as described in the "Getting Started" section of this book. Your Accounts page is also where you'll find any updates to the chapters or to the lesson files. Look on the Lesson & Update Files tab to access the most current content.

In this lesson you'll learn about the different types of fonts that you can use with Adobe Creative Cloud.

Note: If you have not already downloaded the project files for this lesson to your computer from your Account page, make sure you do so now. See "Getting Started" at the beginning of the book.

Choosing font formats for creative projects

Whether you're new to digital fonts or a veteran of print and online publishing, the use of digital fonts has changed dramatically in recent years with new font formats and new ways to use them. Adobe Creative Cloud stays in step with these changes by providing a variety of fonts for print, online, and mobile use.

Fonts for printing

When you apply fonts to text in primarily print-oriented Adobe Creative Cloud software, such as Adobe Photoshop CC or Adobe InDesign CC (or your word processor), you typically use fonts that were designed to be installed and viewed on a desktop or laptop computer. These are the most established kinds of fonts for personal computers and are sometimes called *system fonts* or *desktop fonts*.

Several desktop font formats have been used for print publishing and general personal computer use over the last 20 years. The major font formats of this kind are:

- **PostScript.** The earliest high-quality fonts used for personal-computer-based print publishing were Adobe PostScript fonts. PostScript fonts made it possible to scale type to any size while preserving smooth curves and sharp edges.

- **TrueType.** The most common font format in use today is TrueType, which is now found on just about every Windows and Mac OS X system. TrueType is ubiquitous because it started out as an Apple font format and was later licensed by Microsoft; both companies made TrueType the standard font format for their operating systems.

- **OpenType.** As personal computers and publishing software became more powerful and typographical standards advanced, Microsoft and Adobe worked together to advance type capabilities beyond the limitations of the PostScript and TrueType font formats. This resulted in the OpenType font format, which is an open standard that makes it easier for more companies to create fonts.

A wide variety of inexpensive fonts are available in TrueType format. However, OpenType fonts are now favored by designers and publishers because of advanced typographic capabilities, such as true small caps and old-style figures, and better support for non-English glyphs. (A glyph can be a character or a combination of characters, such as a ligature.) Also, you can use the same font file on Windows and Mac OS X; whereas TrueType or PostScript fonts typically require font files specific to Windows and Mac OS X.

You can use any of these formats in Creative Cloud applications in Windows or Mac OS X. Many fonts are available in all three formats, although new professional fonts are most likely to appear in OpenType format. When you install Creative Cloud applications that support printing, a range of Adobe OpenType fonts are installed along with the application, and those fonts are available to all of the applications on your system.

Fonts for websites

Website projects involve font challenges that don't exist for print. Because website layouts are not fixed, text may be scaled or reflowed as a web page is viewed on differently sized displays or browser windows. This is especially true today because website layouts are increasingly likely to automatically resize for large desktop displays and small tablet and smartphone displays. For website text to reflow as layouts adjust, the font must be present on the device where the website is being displayed. But all fonts are not present on all computers. If you used a font installed on your computer (a system font) in your design, but that font is not on the reader's device, text on your website won't appear as you intended because the reader's web browser will substitute a font that is actually present on the device. Until recently, the solution to this display problem was to specify a font from the limited set installed on most computers, referred to as *web safe* fonts. Of course, using web-safe fonts limits design flexibility because there are so few of them to choose from.

On websites where unique typography was a high priority, other approaches were to convert text to an image or to use browser plug-ins that could support high-quality typography. However, images do not scale smoothly, cannot be searched or highlighted as text, and consume more bandwidth than text, which makes pages load more slowly. The disadvantage of browser plug-ins is that you can't assume they're installed with every web browser, and browser plug-ins are typically not available for mobile web browsers on smartphones and tablets—the fastest-growing area of mobile usage.

Fortunately, those workarounds are no longer necessary because you can now easily use high-quality fonts on websites thanks to advancements in web standards. Current web browsers can now download fonts from servers. So, if a font is not available on the viewing device, that font will simply be downloaded, and the web page text will be displayed as you designed it. In other words, fonts can now be linked by a URL and downloaded, similarly to how you can include images and videos on a web page by embedding URL links to them. The fonts that you can link to are called *web fonts*. When you use web fonts, they're used only temporarily on a site visitor's web browser and don't become available to the rest of the system.

The most common web fonts are available in the following formats:

- **OpenType or TrueType.** It's possible for some web browsers to download the same OpenType and TrueType fonts you would use for print projects, but those fonts are typically not compressed for high performance over networks.

- **Web Open Font Format (WOFF).** A WOFF font can be based on OpenType or TrueType but is optimized for fast downloading.

- **Embedded OpenType (EOT).** An EOT is a compressed Microsoft version of the OpenType font format.

Although you can link to web fonts, you typically do not want to link them to fonts stored on your website the way you store images and other linked content. It's often best to link to fonts provided by a web font service, such as Adobe TypeKit, which is included with your Adobe Creative Cloud subscription. Web font services are useful because there is no font format that works with all web browsers. A web font service can intelligently serve up whichever format works best for the browser that's requesting the fonts. Another good reason to use web font services is that you don't have to worry about font licensing issues; the fonts they serve are cleared for use as downloadable elements of websites.

The only disadvantage of web fonts is that they require up-to-date web browsers. Fortunately, browsers that are incompatible with web fonts are becoming less common and are now found mostly on very old systems. The web browsers on mobile devices typically support web fonts, which makes web fonts a practical and current solution that lets you design websites with access to a wide range of high-quality fonts.

Using fonts with Adobe Creative Cloud

Whether you're designing for print, web, or video, Adobe Creative Cloud makes more fonts accessible to you. When you install Creative Cloud design applications, such as Photoshop CC or InDesign CC, a set of professional OpenType fonts is installed along with the software, and you can use those fonts with any application on your system. These OpenType fonts are system fonts that are appropriate for print projects but are not ideal for text on web pages. For web design projects, you may want to use the Adobe TypeKit web fonts that are included with your Adobe Creative Cloud subscription.

If you build a website by hand coding it, using a web font involves adding appropriate font code in the correct line in your website's CSS code. That isn't necessary when you build your website in designer-friendly Adobe Muse, because the integration of Adobe Muse with Adobe TypeKit lets you choose and apply web fonts to your website by pointing and clicking instead of writing code.

As an additional benefit, some TypeKit fonts are also available for desktop use. When you use the Adobe Creative Cloud desktop application to select TypeKit desktop fonts and sync them to your computer, those fonts are installed on your system and become available to all applications on your system.

In combination, the OpenType fonts installed with Creative Cloud applications and the Creative Cloud access to Adobe TypeKit web and desktop fonts provide you with immediate access to a wide selection of typefaces for your print and web projects.

Choosing desktop fonts in Creative Cloud applications

In Photoshop, InDesign, and other Adobe Creative Cloud design applications, you might notice that the Type menu looks different than it does in other software you may use. The reason is that the Type menu in Creative Cloud software is enhanced to help you choose an appropriate font for your output medium. In applications that are often used for print, the font menu includes a symbol near the font name that indicates the format of each font, like this:

O OpenType

a Adobe PostScript

Tr TrueType

Also, to the right of the font name, you may see a visual sample of the font.

The format of a font does not necessarily guarantee its suitability for a particular purpose, but there are some guidelines you can follow. TrueType fonts are best for printed projects, video, and online presentations. For print projects in which professional typography is a priority, OpenType and PostScript fonts are preferred.

The same font can exist in many versions created by various *type foundries* (companies that design and produce fonts). Some sources of fonts, such as the Adobe Type Library, aspire to higher levels of typographic quality, so their versions of fonts will typically exhibit a high level of quality in subtle design details and may contain additional specialized glyphs. If a font exists in OpenType *and* PostScript formats, the OpenType version will typically be more recent and possibly more refined; however, when you're deciding between multiple versions of the same font, you should always consider the reputation of each type foundry.

Viewing document fonts in Adobe Bridge

You can use Adobe Bridge to inspect the fonts used in some document formats created by Adobe Creative Cloud applications, such as Adobe InDesign and Adobe Illustrator. If Adobe Bridge can display the fonts inside a document, they'll be listed in the Fonts section in the Metadata panel. As a result, you can find out which fonts a document uses without having to open and manually examine it.

Choosing fonts for a website in Adobe Muse

In contrast with print design applications, Adobe Muse was introduced to create website design. Instead of prioritizing fonts that provide the highest quality for print, Muse prioritizes web fonts because you can reasonably expect web fonts to appear as you intended when your website is viewed in current web browsers.

The font menu in Muse contains a Recently Used Fonts section for quick access to fonts you have recently applied. Below that section you'll see three font sections in order of preference for website design:

- **Web Fonts.** The Web Fonts menu offers the largest choice of fonts that you can expect to display as intended when visitors view your website. The fonts in this menu are either present in the open Muse website or added by you, so this menu may be empty if you haven't yet used any web fonts. To customize the Web Fonts menu, see the next section, "Working with Adobe TypeKit web fonts in Adobe Muse."

- **Web Safe Fonts.** Only a small number of fonts are web safe, so they don't provide much design freedom. But because web safe fonts are installed on most devices, if you use one, you can reasonably expect your website to display these fonts as you intended.

- **System Fonts (exports as image).** Muse lists system fonts at the bottom of the menu because they are installed on your computer but probably not on the computers of visitors who view your website, and they are not equipped to be automatically downloaded because they aren't web fonts. If you do choose one of these fonts, Muse converts the text to an image at a fixed size, which is typically not desirable, as described in "Fonts for websites," earlier in this lesson. For all of these reasons, system fonts are the least attractive font choice for websites.

Working with Adobe TypeKit web fonts in Adobe Muse

In Adobe Muse you can apply fonts using a menu in the toolbar or a menu in the Text panel. The items listed in the font menu's Web Fonts section can vary, because that section can contain web fonts used in the currently open document as well as web fonts you've added manually to the menu.

You added and applied a web font in Lesson 3; now you'll take a closer look at the Add Web Fonts dialog box.

1 Make sure your computer is connected to the Internet, and start Adobe Muse CC.

2 In Windows Explorer, Mac OS X Finder, or Adobe Bridge CC, navigate to your Lessons folder, open the Lesson04 folder, and then double-click the file

Pluralist-site-04.muse. The file opens in Adobe Muse CC. If Muse asks you if you want to update links, click Cancel.

3 In the site map, double-click the page Log in/Join to open it in Design view.

4 With the Text tool (T), click a text insertion point anywhere in the Log in/Join text frame. This activates the text options in the Muse toolbar and in the Text panel, including the font menu.

5 Click the font menu in the Muse toolbar or in the Text panel. You'll see two fonts, Frijole and Varela. Both are listed because they are used in the document. Frijole is used on the home page, and Varela is the font used throughout the rest of the site.

If you opened another Muse website that used a different set of web fonts, those would be the fonts listed in the Web Fonts section.

When you want to use web fonts that aren't already listed in the Web Fonts section or when you want to remove unused fonts from the list in the Web Fonts section, you use the Web fonts dialog box.

1   In a font menu, choose Add Web Fonts.

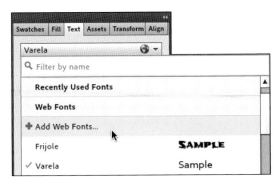

Across the top of the Web Fonts dialog box are controls for viewing the fonts and helping you filter the list to more easily find the fonts you want to add.

2   Click in the Filter By Name field and type **pol**. All of the fonts disappear except for Poller One and Poly because you've just filtered the font list to display only the fonts containing the letters "pol" in the name.

3   Click the Poller One font. A blue check mark appears. The Poller One font is now selected and available in the font menu, but you aren't finished yet. You can add more than one font before you close the Add Web Fonts dialog box.

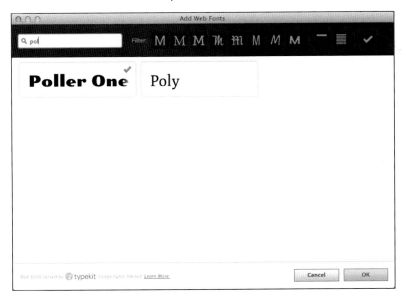

4 Delete the text in the Filter By Name field.

5 Move the mouse over the first icon in the Filter section, and then pause to display the tool tip. It reads "Sans serif: without serifs" to describe which fonts will be displayed if you click the button.

6 Move the mouse over the second icon in the Filter section, and then pause to display the tool tip. It reads "Serif: with serifs" to describe which fonts will be displayed if you click the button.

7 Click the Serif: with Serifs button.

8 Scroll all the way to the bottom of the list of displayed fonts, and click the Ribeye and Tinos fonts to add those to the fonts you've selected.

9 Click the third button from the right; the list now displays just a few fonts. Click the second button from the right to see that a different short list of fonts is displayed. Hover the mouse over each of those buttons to read their tool tips.

Notice that the two buttons you used in step 9 are in their own group. According to the tool tips, the first of the two buttons in that group filters the list for fonts that work well as headings, and the second filters the list for fonts that work well in paragraphs at small sizes. These are only suggestions; you can use a font in any way you like.

10 Click the check mark button at the right end of the filter bar to display fonts you've selected during this session.

The font list may be blank. The reason is that the list displays fonts that meet all the filter criteria, and there may be no selected fonts that match the style, usage, and selection filter buttons that are active.

11 If the heading or paragraph usage button is selected, deselect it. The list should now display the Ribeye and Tinos fonts. You selected one more font earlier, but it isn't displayed because the Serif filter is active.

12 Click the Serif button to deselect it. Now you see all three of the fonts you selected during this session. Poller One wasn't displayed earlier because it is a sans serif font. If there were other web fonts previously added to the Web Fonts section, they would also appear in this list.

13 Click OK. If a Web Fonts Notification alert appears, click OK.

14 Click a font menu. The Poller One, Ribeye, and Tinos fonts are now part of the Web Fonts menu.

15 Choose File > Add/Remove Web Fonts. This is another way to open the Add Web Fonts dialog box.

16 Make sure the Show Selected Fonts button (the check mark button) is selected, and click the Ribeye font. It becomes deselected and disappears.

17 Click OK. If a Web Fonts Notification alert appears, click OK.

18 Click a font menu, and notice that Ribeye is no longer available.

Congratulations! You've learned how to work with web fonts in Adobe Muse. Now you can apply a wide range of Adobe TypeKit fonts to your websites and be confident that they'll display as you intended in current web browsers.

Wrapping up

Adobe Creative Cloud greatly simplifies the process of choosing appropriate fonts for design projects that target different media. You can take advantage of the fonts installed with Creative Cloud for your print, video, and interactive projects. If you design websites with Adobe Muse, you can easily add and use a wide range of web fonts for design flexibility.

Review questions

1   What are the three font formats traditionally used for print publishing and general computer use?

2   How can you find out which fonts were used in an Adobe InDesign or Adobe Illustrator document without opening the document?

3   What are the three types of fonts that can potentially be specified for text on a web page?

4   Of the three types of fonts you can potentially specify for web page text, which one is the best and for what two reasons?

5   How do you add or remove web fonts from the font menu in Adobe Muse?

Review answers

1   OpenType, PostScript, and TrueType are the three font formats traditionally used for print publishing and general computer use.

2   Select an Adobe InDesign or Adobe Illustrator file in Adobe Bridge, and look at the Fonts section in the Metadata panel.

3   Web fonts, web safe fonts, and system fonts can potentially be specified for text on a web page.

4   Web fonts are the best choice for websites because they provide a wider range of font choices than web safe fonts and can be automatically downloaded to a website visitor's web browser.

5   Click Add Fonts in the font menu or choose File > Add/Remove Web Fonts to open the Add Web Fonts dialog box. In the dialog box you can choose from all fonts available in Adobe TypeKit.

5 CREATING A VIDEO WITH PHOTOSHOP

Lesson overview

You can use the Timeline panel in Adobe Photoshop CC to create video by assembling media using cuts, fades, and transitions without having to learn additional software. This makes it easy for you to create video for projects such as your website or an app for the iPad. This lesson will introduce you to important skills and concepts:

- Organizing media for your video
- Using the Timeline panel
- Creating a video slide show using images and text
- Animating layers
- Using audio
- Exporting video

You'll probably need about two hours to complete this lesson. Download the project files for this lesson from the Lesson & Update Files tab on your Account page at www.peachpit.com and store them on your computer in a convenient location, as described in the "Getting Started" section of this book. Your Accounts page is also where you'll find any updates to the chapters or to the lesson files. Look on the Lesson & Update Files tab to access the most current content.

In this lesson, you'll use Adobe Photoshop CC to create, edit, and export a promotional video slide show with animated layers.

Note: If you have not already downloaded the project files for this lesson to your computer from your Account page, make sure you do so now. See "Getting Started" at the beginning of the book.

Setting up

In earlier lessons you've used Adobe Bridge to browse assets for print and web projects. Because of its broad file format support, you can use Adobe Bridge to browse and organize movie files, animation files, audio files, still images, and other similar content for your video projects. In this lesson you'll use Adobe Bridge to preview the image candidates for the video and pick out four final images.

1 Start Adobe Bridge, and make sure the Essentials workspace is selected at the top of the Adobe Bridge window.

2 Make sure the Adobe Bridge window is set to Sort by Filename and in ascending order. You can verify this by choosing View > Sort or by looking at the sort controls below the search field at the top-right corner of the Adobe Bridge window.

Tip: If the thumbnail images are hard to see, drag the zoom slider at the bottom of the Adobe Bridge window or press Ctrl-+/ Command-+.

3 Navigate to the Lesson05 folder on your hard drive, and double-click the folder Video Candidates. You'll see eight images, a mix of TIFF, JPEG, and Photoshop formats. You can see a full-screen preview of any of the photos by pressing the spacebar while an image is selected.

Now you'll quickly evaluate the eight available images and narrow down the set to the four final images you'll actually use in the video.

4 Choose Edit > Select All (Ctrl-A/Command-A).

5 Choose View > Review Mode (Ctrl-B/Command-B).

In Review Mode, Adobe Bridge displays the images as a full-screen carousel. Review Mode provides tools for rapidly rating, labeling, and rejecting images so that you can efficiently reduce many candidates down to a final set.

Note: You can use camera raw format images, but when you bring them into Photoshop, Adobe Camera Raw will appear so you can convert them for use in Photoshop.

6 Click the left arrow or right arrow buttons at the bottom-left corner of the screen, or press the left arrow and right arrow keys on your keyboard. Adobe Bridge cycles through the selected images. Stop when you've seen all eight images.

The video needs images that will have a dynamic feel when animated, so you'll evaluate them in turn and reject the weakest images until four images remain.

7 Using the arrow buttons or the left arrow/right arrow keys, rotate the carousel to display the image Waterfall_Shot06_0105. This is an example of a shot that would work well in the video because it implies motion, and there's room to pan across it without hitting the edge of the frame, so you'll keep it.

8 Rotate the carousel to the right to display the image Zipline_Shot02_0846.tif. This image will also be useful, so rotate again to the next image, 4x4_Shot01_0529.jpg.

9 Although the shot of the sport utility vehicle is dynamic, it's best if the video focuses on people, so you'll deselect this shot. Click the down arrow button in the bottom-left corner of the screen, or press the down arrow key. The image disappears, but it's only deselected, not deleted.

   After the previous image is deselected, the next image (Beach_Kayak_Shot04_0511.jpg) becomes the currently displayed image.

10 The kayak image is dynamic but fills so much of the frame that there won't be much room for animation without losing much of the subject. Deselect this image too, using the down arrow button or down arrow key.

   After the previous image is deselected, the next image (Beach_Shot02_0012.psd) becomes the currently displayed image. This photo would make a good final image for the video and can be zoomed during playback, so you'll keep it.

11 Rotate the carousel one image to the right. The next image, Campsite_Shot01_0105.jpg, is not dynamic and doesn't contain people, so deselect it.

The next image (Hiking_Shot05_0332.psd) fits the criteria, but you have five images and you need only four. There's just one image you haven't examined yet so you'll look at that one now.

12 Rotate the carousel one image to the right. The image Hiking_Shot05_0347.tif is more dramatic than the previous image and has potential for animation, so you'll keep this one and deselect the previous one.

13 Rotate the carousel to the left to display the image Hiking_Shot05_0332.psd, and deselect it.

Adobe Bridge displays the four remaining images, but now they display as a grid, not a carousel. Adobe Bridge displays images as a carousel only when there are more than four.

Because all you did was deselect the images you didn't want, they're not marked in any way and you won't be able to tell which images were picked when these images become deselected at some point after you exit Review Mode. You can mark these images in many ways, such as using the keyboard shortcuts for star ratings or labels, but another way is to put them in their own collection.

A collection is a way to organize files in Adobe Bridge without having to move or copy the originals, because a collection is merely virtual, a list that refers to files in folders. This means a collection can contain files from different folders. You'll create a collection in Review Mode.

14 Click the New Collection button near the bottom-right corner of the screen; then in the New Collection dialog box, enter **Video Images** and click Save.

Adobe Bridge exits Review Mode, and now the Content view displays only the four images you kept; however, they are now displayed inside their collection, not their folder. In the Collections tab (Window > Collections), you see the new collection you just created.

▶ **Tip:** To return to the folder containing the original images, select any image in the collection and choose File > Reveal in Bridge.

With the original set of images narrowed down to four final images, you're ready to start assembling the images into a video in Photoshop.

Video in the Creative Cloud

As more projects move from print to the screen, and as high-definition video playback becomes common on even the most portable devices, video is an increasingly common element on websites, in apps, and in interactive presentations. Although the video-editing features in Adobe Photoshop CC aren't intended to replace full-featured video-editing software, such as Adobe Premiere Pro CC, Photoshop does provide tools for the kinds of video content you might want to include in creative projects, and they're designed to fit right in with the familiar Photoshop user interface. This makes Photoshop a great place to get started editing video.

As you become experienced editing video with Photoshop, you may have ideas for video that go beyond the capabilities of Photoshop. For example, you may want to edit program-length, broadcast-ready videos or create advanced video effects. When that happens, your Adobe Creative Cloud subscription gives you the option to move up to Adobe Premiere Pro for video editing and Adobe After Effects for video effects whenever you are ready. Adobe Premiere Pro and After Effects are not covered in this book because their workflows and user interface are designed to be familiar to video professionals, whereas this book focuses on workflows for designers. But Adobe Premiere Pro and After Effects represent a Creative Cloud path that you can follow when you want to grow your video skills further.

Let's take a look at a finished version of the video you'll create today. In the Lesson05 folder, double-click the file Pluralist video final.mp4, and when it opens play it back. It's about ten seconds long and includes four still photos that are animated and an audio track playing in the background. At the end a text layer appears and zooms.

Starting a Photoshop video document

Although you can create a video of any size, for this project you'll create one that fits the standard 16:9 aspect ratio of high definition televisions so that it can be displayed either on a website or on its own on an HDTV.

Creating a new Photoshop video document

1   In Photoshop, choose File > New, and then in the New Document dialog box enter **My Pluralist Video** for the Name.

2   Choose Film & Video from the Preset menu.

3   Choose HDTV 1080p/29.97, a common widescreen television format.

    You aren't locked into this size; when you finish the video, you can export to another size. It's best to edit at the largest size you think you'll need and simply downsize it at export time.

4   Click OK.

Tip: You can also start a video document by opening a video clip directly in Photoshop instead of creating a new document. The new Photoshop document will use the exact pixel dimensions of that video, and you can then add more videos and stills to that document.

5 Choose the Motion workspace from the workspace menu in the Options bar, or choose Window > Workspace > Motion. The most noticeable effect of applying this workspace is that the Timeline panel becomes available at the bottom of the Photoshop workspace. You can also show or hide the Timeline panel by choosing Window > Timeline, or by double-clicking the Timeline panel tab.

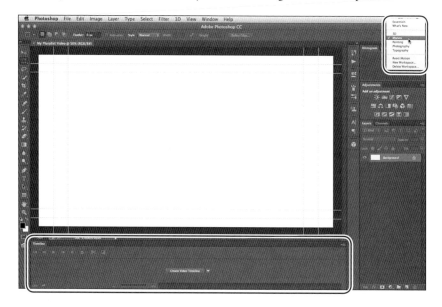

Tip: You don't have to import from Adobe Bridge. You can drag and drop media into Photoshop from other applications that support standard dragging and dropping.

6 Choose File > Save As, navigate to the Lesson05 folder, and click Save.

Adding media to Photoshop

The collection you created earlier in Adobe Bridge will now come in handy because all of the media you want to use are in one place. You're now ready to add the media to Photoshop. This is as easy as dragging and dropping between the two applications.

1 In the Timeline panel, click the Create Video Timeline button.

Creating a video timeline, or sequence, in the Timeline panel enables the features that make video editing possible in Photoshop.

2 Arrange the Adobe Bridge and Photoshop windows so that you can see both.

Creative Cloud video tools

If you decide to become more deeply involved in video production, Adobe Creative Cloud provides a complete set of professional tools for video editing, video production, and motion graphics:

- Adobe Premiere Pro CC is fast, efficient, professional, video editing software.

- Adobe After Effects CC software provides cinematic visual effects and motion graphics.

- Adobe Audition CC lets you record, mix, and restore audio, especially for use as audio tracks in a video project.

- Adobe SpeedGrade CC provides advanced tools for *color grading*—the process of balancing color across your video clips and creating a distinctive color look for your video productions.

- Adobe Story CC Plus combines screenwriting features with powerful scheduling and reporting tools. You may find Story to be useful for scripting and organizing the production schedules of videos you create, particularly with a team.

- Adobe Prelude CC optimizes the process of ingesting video clips to your computer and logging them in order to streamline your production workflow. For example, Prelude can help you link clips to scenes in a script and add metadata (such as locations, scene names, and actor names) that you can use to find clips quickly.

- Adobe Media Encoder CC optimizes video for any screen size and resolution. It works with many Creative Cloud applications to render finished video quickly and efficiently, and it supports a wide range of formats from smartphones to theater movies.

- Adobe Encore lets you create DVDs, Blu-ray Discs, and web DVDs, including menu navigation.

You may also find some of these tools to be useful for capturing or preparing clips for use in a Photoshop video project.

3 In Adobe Bridge, select all of the images in the Video Images collection and drag them into the Photoshop document window.

▶ **Tip:** If you're mixing stills, videos, and video sizes, you can save steps by making sure that the first file you drag into Photoshop (with no documents open) is the video matching the pixel dimensions of the video you want to create. This automatically creates a new document at the optimal size and creates a video Timeline and video group.

4 Because you made the Photoshop window smaller to drag and drop with Adobe Bridge, enlarge or maximize the size of the Photoshop window to a comfortable size for you to work.

You see your first image on the Photoshop document with a Free Transform bounding box and handles. This means the image is not yet fully placed in the document; the bounding box is there to give you an opportunity to move and resize the object first.

5 Click the aspect ratio lock icon in the Options bar, and in the W field type **1920px** (the width of the video document); then press Enter/Return. This action fits the object in the document without leaving empty areas.

6 Press Enter/Return to finish placing the first image, deselecting it.

7 The next image appears with its Free Transform bounding box; repeat steps 5 and 6 for that image and the last two until all of the images you dragged in are placed.

8 Save the document. If the Photoshop Format Options dialog box appears, click OK.

The images you imported appear in the Layers panel, which is what you'd expect from working with stills in Photoshop. However, the same stack of layers also appears in the Timeline panel; next you'll turn that stack into a sequence in time.

Note: Keep in mind that you're not finished adding documents until you've pressed Enter/Return for the last video or still image you imported.

Building a video sequence

The video features in Photoshop give you the essentials of video integrated into the way Photoshop already works. This simplifies the video editing learning curve for designers and photographers. You'll start with the video group you created after importing files.

Although you're creating a video from still images in this lesson, you can apply the same techniques when you edit video clips. Photoshop can easily handle clips from video cameras, smartphones, and digital SLRs that can shoot video.

Tip: If you later add a new layer to a video group and it seems to be invisible on the canvas, move the current-time indicator so that it's within that layer in the sequence.

About the Timeline panel

You'll use the Timeline panel to string together still images into a sequence. You'll also find more video-related commands in the Layer > Video Layers submenu.

On the Canvas, by default you see a set of blue guides near the edge. These were added by the new document preset you chose when you created the document. The outer guides mark the *action-safe* area, and the inner guides mark the *title-safe* area. The idea behind these is that many televisions slightly enlarge and crop the video image, a practice known as *overscan*. If you want to make sure that important video subjects and text do not get cut off on TVs that overscan, keep important subjects inside the action-safe area and keep all text inside the title-safe area.

Think of the Timeline panel as a time-based version of the Layers panel; you see the same layers stacked from front (top) to back (bottom) in both panels. The difference in the Timeline panel is that you can create a video group that also sequences layers in time. You can freely mix static layers with video groups, and a layer you use in a video group can be a video, still image, or any other layer you can create in Photoshop, such as text or a background. In addition, you can animate any layer. The next step in this lesson is to create a video group from the media you imported.

▶ **Tip:** The main difference between video layers and video groups is that a video group can contain multiple layers sequenced in time.

1 In the Timeline panel, Shift-click the first and last layers you imported (don't include Layer 0), click the filmstrip icon on any of the selected layers, and choose New Video Group from Clips. The layers appear as a new video group in the Timeline panel and also in the Layers panel.

Photoshop sequences the layers in time, one after the other. From here, you can reorder the layers, adjust when they start and end, and apply corrections and effects.

2 In the Timeline panel, adjust the Timeline magnification so that you can see the entire video group sequence.

You won't need Layer 0, so you can delete it.

3 Click the filmstrip icon for Layer 0 and choose Delete Track.

▶ **Tip:** You can also delete a layer by pressing the Delete key when the layer is selected in the Timeline panel or Layers panel.

4 Save the document.

Previewing the Timeline panel

Previewing high-definition video can be a challenge for some computer systems, so there is a chance that playback may not be smooth when you preview the sequence. The speed of video playback is also affected by the number and nature of effects you apply to video, the frame rate of video clips, and the pixel dimensions of the frame.

1 Press the spacebar. Let the sequence play back until it reaches the end of the last image.

2 Click the Go To First Frame button (![button]( )) to return to the beginning of the sequence.

Photoshop previews only the *work area*, which is indicated by the vertical work area bars in the Timeline panel. A smaller work area takes less work and time for a computer to preview. The larger the work area, the more RAM is required to keep all of the rendered preview frames in memory.

If your system isn't fast enough to play back frames smoothly, you can lower the preview resolution until you see smooth playback. This doesn't affect the resolution of the original files or the export resolution, so you can change it at any time depending on how you want to set the balance between playback smoothness and preview detail.

To adjust playback resolution, click the gear button in the Timeline panel playback controls and choose a percentage from the Resolution menu. For example, 50% means the sequence will play back at 50% of the document resolution.

Making edits

By default, video clips are the duration that they were when you imported them, and still images are 5 seconds long. For this video, each image needs to be about 2.5 seconds long (2:15 or two seconds fifteen frames) so you'll adjust each image's duration now. These aren't the final durations, but they are a better starting point than the default five-second duration.

1   Position the pointer over the right side of the first layer in the sequence and drag to the left until the Duration in the tool tip reads 2:15.

Although a video clip can't be longer than its original duration, you can show a still image for as long or as short a time as you like. When you adjust duration by a certain amount, all of the media that follows moves forward or back by that amount; this is known as a *ripple edit*.

Tip: If you have difficulty controlling the duration precisely, magnify the Timeline panel using the slider at the bottom of the Timeline panel. Also, holding down the Ctrl/ Control key can help because it overrides snapping behavior as you drag.

2   Repeat step 1 for the next three images, setting each of them to a duration of 2:15.

3   Play back the sequence to preview the new durations.

The current sequence is not the desired final sequence, but it's easy to rearrange the order of the images. You may need to magnify the Timeline to see the layer names.

1   In the Timeline panel, drag the layer Waterfall_Shot06_0105 and drop it at the beginning of the sequence. As you drag, a black vertical bar appears where the layer will be positioned if you release the mouse; so drop the image when you see a black bar appear before (not after) the first image.

2   Drag the image Zipline_Shot02_0846 and drop it so that it's the second image in the sequence.

3   Drag the image Hiking_Shot05_0347 and drop it so that it's the third image in the sequence.

The image Beach_Shot02_0012 should now be the last image in the sequence.

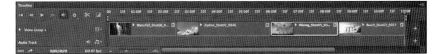

4   Play back the sequence to preview the new sequence of images.

5   Save the document.

Video layers inside a video group are always sequenced with the other layers in that video group. If you want a still or video clip to play in front of or behind other layers (in the stacking order, not in time), drag that layer out of a video group and stack it by itself in the Layers panel or into another layer group. That layer will no longer be affected by the edits inside the video group.

Adding transitions and fades

Although transitions can add visual interest to a video project, the majority of television programs, movies, and commercials tell their stories using simple cuts and fades. For this reason, the basic set of transitions in Photoshop should be sufficient for most projects. You'll add crossfades between the images in the video you're creating in Photoshop.

1 In the Timeline panel, click the Add Transition button and select Cross Fade.

2 Enter **.3** for the Duration. This value, in seconds, sets the default duration for the transitions you're about to add.

▶ **Tip:** Dragging a transition does not automatically close the Add Transition menu, so if you leave it open, you can drag multiple transitions from it without having to reopen the list of transitions.

3 Drag a Cross Fade transition and drop it on the edit point between the first two layers in the sequence. A transition will snap to an edit point as you drag over it.

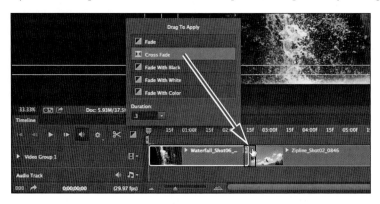

Video playback and cached frames

To display frames as quickly as possible, Photoshop caches frames in RAM. You can tell which frames are cached by looking at the teal-colored bar that appears above the sequence when you preview. If the video is playing back at the Timeline's frame rate, the teal bar is solid and the frame rate at the bottom of the sequence is white. If the computer can't keep up, the frame rate readout is red and the teal bar has breaks in it to indicate which frames weren't cached.

You can cache uncached frames by playing the sequence again with audio muted and Allow Frame Skipping turned off in the Timeline panel menu. This forces Photoshop to cache every frame, because it won't be skipping frames to keep video in sync with real-time audio playback. Just remember to unmute audio and turn on Allow Frame Skipping when you're done.

If there isn't enough RAM to cache all the frames, you'll see earlier frames become uncached to free up space. In other words, the teal line won't extend all the way across and there will always be a gap that's never closed. To prevent this, make the work area smaller until the teal line stays completely solid. If this happens often, you'll need to give Photoshop more RAM by closing other applications or adding more RAM. You can also increase the memory allocated to Photoshop in the Performance panel in the Preferences dialog box, as long as you don't exceed the Ideal Range listed there (you must leave some RAM free for your operating system).

4 Repeat step 3 to create the same transition at the edit points between the other layers.

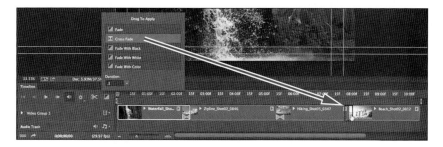

5 Play back the sequence to preview the transitions.

Now you can fade in the beginning of the video and fade out the end. You'll fade in from black and fade out to white, but first you'll adjust the overall duration of the sequence.

1   In the Timeline panel, drag the end of the last layer (Beach_Shot02_0012) so that the tool tip reads "End: 10:00" (ten seconds).

2   Click the Add Transition button and drag a Fade With Black transition to the beginning of the sequence.

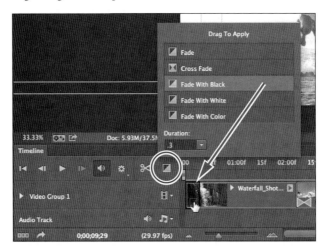

3   Drag a Fade With White transition to the end of the sequence.

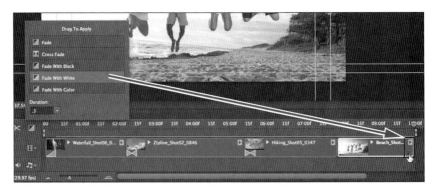

The fade at the end of the sequence is intended to be long, so you'll extend it.

4 Position the pointer at the beginning of the Fade With White transition and drag to the left until the tool tip reads "Duration: 1:00."

Adding a logo from Illustrator

The video will end with the Pluralist logo over the last image, so you'll import that now. The logo was drawn in Adobe Illustrator, which means it's vector artwork that won't appear jaggy when scaled up; it stays sharp when scaled to any size.

1 In Photoshop choose Select > Deselect Layers. (If the command is unavailable, you don't need to select it.)

2 In the Timeline panel, Shift-drag to snap the current-time indicator to the edit point between the third and fourth images.

3 Arrange the Adobe Bridge and Photoshop windows so that you can see both of them.

4 In Adobe Bridge, select any of the images in the Video Images collection and choose File > Reveal in Bridge to return to the Video Candidates folder; then click Lesson05 in the path bar to go up one level to the lesson folder.

5　Drag the file Pluralist_logo_video.ai to the center of the Photoshop canvas and drop it. If the Place PDF dialog box appears, click OK.

6　Press Enter/Return to apply the Transform bounding box because you can place the file at its current size and position. The logo is a vector object that was created in Adobe Illustrator, so you can resize it freely without loss of quality.

7　Change the size of the Photoshop window so that it's a comfortable size for you to work.

In the Timeline panel, the Pluralist_logo_video file was added as its own video group. The reason is that you deselected all layers in step 1. If you had left Video Group 1 selected, the logo would have been added to the end of that video group.

The logo will be animated over the final image, but you can see that the logo doesn't stand out very well. You'll add a glow effect to increase the visual separation of the logo from the background.

8　With the Pluralist_logo_video layer selected in the Layers panel, click the Add A Layer Style button at the bottom of the Layers panel and choose Outer Glow.

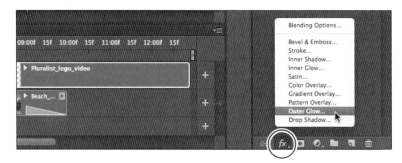

9 In the Outer Glow section of the Layer Style dialog box, make sure Blend Mode is set to Screen, a light yellow color is selected, Opacity is set to 90%, Spread is set to 0%, and Size is set to 100px.

10 In the Outer Glow section of the Layer Style dialog box, click the Contour button, and then click the first option in the second row.

The logo now stands out much better against the background.

11 Click OK to close the Layer Style dialog box, and save the document.

Panning and zooming

In the Photoshop video Timeline, over time you can animate position and other transformation attributes, layer opacity, and layer style attributes. For this lesson you'll concentrate on panning (animating layer position) and zooming (animating layer size).

Photoshop offers two ways to animate layers. Choosing a preset is quick and easy; you can also animate with keyframes for more manual control over how an attribute changes over time.

Animating with presets

The first three images in the sequence will simply pan across the screen. You can quickly and easily accomplish this using the Pan motion preset in the Timeline panel.

1   In the Timeline panel, click the arrow at the top-right corner of the image Waterfall_Shot06_0105 and choose Pan from the Motion menu.

2 Enter **–55** in the Pan option, select Resize to Fill Canvas, and press Enter/ Return to close the Motion options.

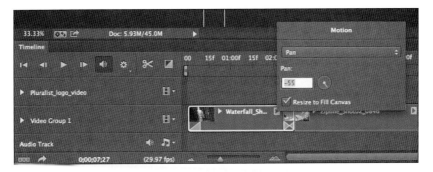

In the Motion options, the Pan angle sets the direction of the panning motion, and the Resize to Fill Canvas option ensures that the image will not leave empty areas of the canvas.

3 Click the Go To First Frame button and play back the sequence to preview the effect you applied to Waterfall_Shot06_0105.

Playback may be slower than real time the first time you preview the layer as Photoshop caches the rendered frames (see the sidebar "Video playback and cached frames" earlier in the chapter). When the teal bar is solid, indicating fully rendered frames, the sequence plays back in real time as long as your computer is fast enough to do so.

4 Click the arrow at the top-right corner of the image Zipline_Shot02_0846 and choose Pan & Zoom from the Motion menu.

5 Enter **18** in the Pan option, select Zoom In from the Zoom menu, select Resize to Fill Canvas, and press Enter/Return to close the Motion options.

6 Click the arrow at the top-right corner of the image Hiking_Shot05_0347 and choose Pan from the Motion menu.

7 Enter **–180** in the Pan option, select Resize to Fill Canvas, and press Enter/Return to close the Motion options.

8 Click the Go To First Frame button and play back the sequence to preview the effects you applied to the first three images.

For Hiking_Shot05_0347, the layer pans from right to left because the Pan angle is negative. When the Pan angle is positive, the layer moves from left to right.

Animating with keyframes

When you need more control over animation than the presets provide, you can use keyframes in the Timeline panel instead. A keyframe is a marker that indicates a change in animation; you need to set at least two keyframes to define an animation. For example, if you want to zoom a photo, you create a keyframe at the start and stop times of the animation, and also set the zoom value at each keyframe. Each keyframe remembers its setting, and Photoshop interpolates the transition over time between the keyframes.

You'll use keyframes to precisely zoom the final layer in the sequence and the logo.

1 Shift-drag the current-time indicator to snap it to the edit point between the third and last layers in Video Group 1.

2 Click the triangle to the left of the layer name Beach_Shot02_0012 to reveal the keyframe controls. The colored shading below the layer indicates that you're editing keyframes for that layer only, not for the entire sequence.

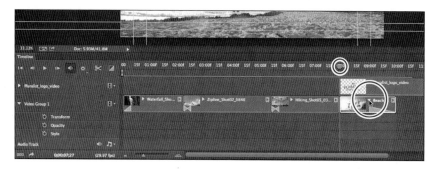

3 Click the stopwatch icon for the Transform attribute to enable keyframe
   animation and add a yellow keyframe at the current-time indicator.

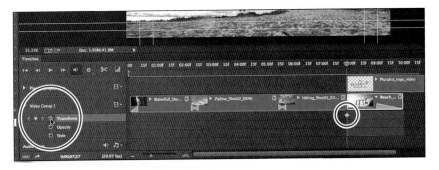

4 Position the current-time indicator at the 9:00 mark, which is the beginning of
   the fade transition you added to the end of the Beach_Shot02_0012 layer.

5 Click the Add or Remove Keyframe At Playhead button (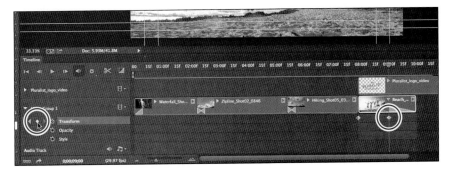) to add a keyframe
   at the current-time indicator.

6 Select the layer Beach_Shot02_0012 and choose Edit > Free Transform (Ctrl-T/
   Command-T).

7 In the Options bar, select the Maintain Aspect Ratio button, enter **3600px** for
   W (width), and press Enter/Return. Press Enter/Return again to exit the Free
   Transform bounding box.

8 Preview the animation for the last layer.

The first keyframe recorded the original layer scaling, and the second keyframe recorded the maximum layer scaling (3600px wide). Photoshop calculates the size of the layer at each frame between the first and second keyframes.

Now you'll scale the logo over time in a similar way, but instead of scaling it up you'll scale it down.

1 Click the triangle to the left of the layer name Pluralist_logo_video to reveal the keyframe controls and the colored shading below the layer.

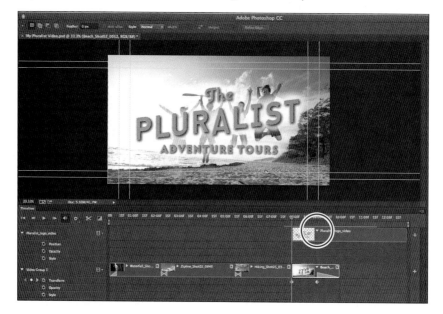

Notice that although the Beach_Shot02_0012 layer you already animated has a keyframe control for Transform, Pluralist_logo_video has a keyframe control for Position instead. This means you can't currently animate scaling, which is a Transform attribute instead of simply the layer position. To have the layer display the same Transform attributes as the other layers, you'll need to apply a Smart Object conversion, even if the layer already appears to be a Smart Object. (The images were automatically converted to Smart Objects when you imported them into a video group.)

▶ **Tip:** The Convert to Smart Object command is also available when you right-click/Control-click a layer in the Layers panel.

2 Select the layer Pluralist_logo_video and choose Layer > Smart Objects > Convert to Smart Object. In the Layers panel, the icon for the layer changes to indicate that it is now a Smart Object.

3 Click the triangle to the left of the layer name Pluralist_logo_video to reveal the keyframe controls and the shading below the layer, and notice that in the

Timeline panel the Position attribute for the logo layer now reads Transform. You can now animate the scaling of the layer.

First you'll set the duration of the logo layer to match up with the rest of the sequence.

4   Drag the end of the Pluralist_logo_video layer so that it ends at 10:00, the same time as the Video Group 1 sequence.

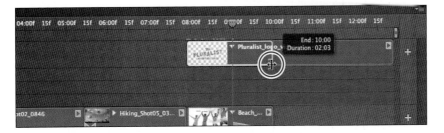

5   Position the current-time indicator at the 9:00 mark; the current-time indicator should snap to the beginning of the fade transition you added to the Beach_ Shot02_0012 layer.

6   Click the stopwatch icon for the Transform attribute for the Pluralist_logo_ video, enabling keyframe animation. Clicking the stopwatch icon also adds a keyframe that records the current size of the layer at that frame.

7   Position the current-time indicator at the beginning of the Pluralist_logo_video layer.

8   Click the Add or Remove Keyframe At Playhead button to add a keyframe at the current-time indicator.

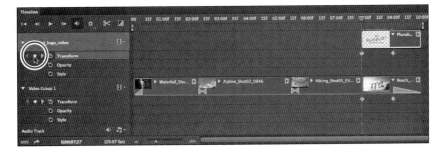

9   Select the layer Pluralist_logo_video and choose Edit > Free Transform (Ctrl-T/ Command-T).

10 In the Options bar, select the Maintain Aspect Ratio button, enter **3800px** for W (width), and press Enter/Return. Press Enter/Return again to exit the Free Transform bounding box.

11 Preview the animation for the last layer.

12 Click the triangles to the left of the Pluralist_logo_video and Video Group 1 tracks to hide the keyframe displays.

13 Save your work.

Using audio

If video clips in a sequence contain audio, Photoshop plays the audio. In this lesson you've been creating a slide show from images, so there is no audio so far. You'll now add music to the sequence.

There's one audio track in the Timeline panel by default, but you can add more at anytime. Controls in the Timeline panel let you add audio clips to a track.

1   At the bottom of the Timeline panel, click the musical notes icon in the Audio
    Track and choose Add Audio.

2   Navigate to the Lesson05 folder, select Pluralist_Audio.aiff, and click Open.
    The audio appears in the Audio Track.

    The audio is longer than the video, so you'll want to trim it and fade it out.
    You can do this using controls that you access much like you did for the video
    motion presets.

3   Drag the right edge of the Pluralist_Audio.aiff clip so that it ends at the same
    time as the video.

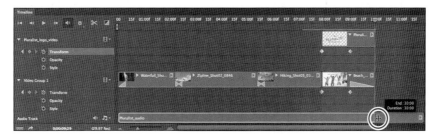

4   Click the triangle at the right edge of the Pluralist_Audio clip. Notice that the
    audio options include Volume, Fade In, Fade Out, and Mute.

5   Enter 1 for Fade Out, and press Enter/Return to close the audio options.

▶ Tip: If the audio for your video project requires more extensive editing than is available in Photoshop, you can edit the audio by downloading and using Adobe Audition CC, which is powerful audio editing software that's included with your Creative Cloud subscription.

If you need to mute audio while editing, you have two choices. Each track provides a mute icon to the left of the musical notes icon, or you can silence all tracks by deselecting the mute icon that appears after the playback controls.

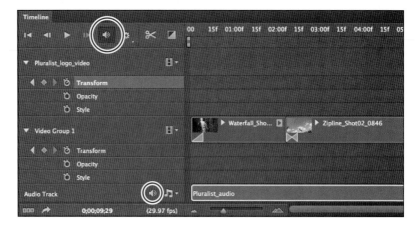

6 Preview the sequence to hear the audio.

7 Save your work.

Exporting video

Photoshop greatly simplifies the process of exporting video to a format you can upload to a service such as YouTube or Vimeo, or add to a website or mobile app. Although many video exporting utilities contain numerous and complex options for rendering exported video, Photoshop provides high-quality, easy-to-use presets based on the most common uses for video today.

1 Click the Render Video button.

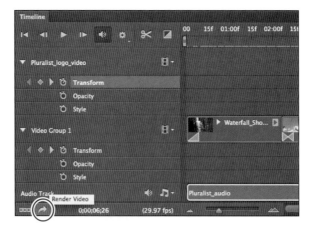

2 For Name, enter **MyPluralistVideo**.

3 Click Select Folder and navigate to the Lesson05 folder.

4 In the next section, choose Adobe Media Encoder. (Photoshop Image Sequence is intended for animations.) Adobe Media Encoder is the same technology used by Adobe Premiere Pro and other professional video applications that are part of Creative Cloud.

5 For Format, choose H.264.

6 For Preset, choose YouTube HD 1080p 29.97.

This preset is suitable for uploading to YouTube in high definition 1080p resolution. You don't have to change any more options in this section of the Render Video dialog box because choosing a preset configures them for you.

Each Format choice provides a different set of presets, so if you can't find a preset you were expecting, make sure you've chosen the proper Format. For most uses on websites, mobile media, and social media, you'll typically choose H.264 as the Format and then choose a preset based on your specific output.

7 Click OK. Photoshop renders the video as it exports it to a file.

8 Save your work.

9 Switch to the desktop and find the file you exported. You can play it back in a standard video player to see how it turned out.

Wrapping up

Congratulations! You've learned how to create a dynamic, high-definition slide show using Photoshop and other Creative Cloud tools. You also learned how to export the video to different media, and you'll use the video you exported in the next lesson.

Review questions

1 In Adobe Bridge, what features of Review Mode make it valuable for narrowing down the best content for a project?

2 What's the difference between a video layer and a video group?

3 What are some steps you can take if video previewing doesn't play back smoothly?

4 How do you change the duration of a transition?

5 What are the two ways to apply motion to a layer, and what's the difference between them?

Review answers

1 Review Mode lets you compare selected images, deselect the ones you don't want to use, and create a collection of the ones you want to keep.

2 A video layer is like a normal Photoshop layer included in a video, whereas the layers in a video group can be sequenced in time.

3 Try reducing the playback resolution, making more RAM available by closing other programs, adding RAM to the computer, or using a smaller work area in the Timeline panel.

4 To change the duration of a transition, drag the beginning or end of the transition in the Timeline panel.

5 You can apply a motion preset, or you can control motion using keyframes. Presets are easy but provide few options, whereas keyframes take more time to set up manually but provide much more control.

6 CREATING AN IPAD APP

Lesson overview

In this lesson you'll learn essential skills and techniques that will help you convert a printed brochure to a mobile format:

- Adding interactivity and navigation

- Adding video

- Creating alternate layouts for different orientations and screen sizes

- Testing an iPad app

You'll probably need between one and two hours to complete this lesson. Download the project files for this lesson from the Lesson & Update Files tab on your Account page at www.peachpit.com and store them on your computer in a convenient location, as described in the "Getting Started" section of this book. Your Accounts page is also where you'll find any updates to the chapters or to the lesson files. Look on the Lesson & Update Files tab to access the most current content.

Learn how to create an iPad app using Adobe
InDesign CC and Adobe Digital Publishing Suite,
Single Edition without any programming. Add
interactive elements and video to the document,
and then test it on an iPad.

Note: If you
have not already
downloaded the project
files for this lesson
to your computer
from your Account
page, make sure
you do so now. See
"Getting Started" at the
beginning of the book.

Setting up InDesign to use Digital Publishing Suite

Your Adobe Creative Cloud subscription includes Digital Publishing Suite (DPS), Single Edition, which lets you create an unlimited number of iPad apps. (Other versions of DPS let you create apps for smartphones and other tablets; see the sidebar "Creating apps for other tablets and smartphones.") Digital Publishing Suite provides tools that integrate with Adobe InDesign CC so that you can use the powerful design and production tools in InDesign to create the iPad app. After you create the content and interactivity with InDesign, Digital Publishing Suite can build the app.

Note: Although you
can use DPS to create
an unlimited number
of iPad apps, there are
additional steps and
requirements involved
in distributing the app
through the Apple App
Store. See the sidebar
"Publishing your app
through a store" later in
this lesson.

Before you start creating an iPad app, make sure you've got the latest versions of InDesign and DPS SE.

1 Start InDesign CC and choose Help > Updates.

2 If any updates are available for InDesign CC, install them.

It's also a good idea to set up your InDesign workspace with the panels that will be the most useful to you. You'll do this in the InDesign publication that you'll be working with during this lesson.

1 Start Adobe Bridge.

2 Navigate to the Lesson06 folder on your hard drive and double-click the file iPadApp_Start.indt to open it.

Creating apps for other tablets and smartphones

You can use InDesign to create apps for tablets and smartphones other than the Apple iPad. This chapter focuses on the iPad because your Creative Cloud subscription includes Adobe Digital Publishing Suite, Single Edition, which lets you create an unlimited number of apps for the iPad only. Creating apps for other tablets and smartphones requires using Adobe Digital Publishing Suite, Enterprise Edition or Adobe Digital Publishing Suite, Professional Edition. The Enterprise and Professional Editions are not part of Creative Cloud and require additional fees.

Also, keep in mind that although Adobe Digital Publishing Suite lets you create and test apps, the process of submitting apps to various app stores and having them accepted is controlled by those app stores and therefore outside the scope of Adobe Digital Publishing Suite. For more information, see the sidebar "Publishing your app through a store" later in this chapter.

3   Choose File > Save. In the Save As dialog box, navigate to the Lesson06 folder, name the document **Wild Isles iPad.indd**, choose InDesign CC document from the Save As Type/Format menu, and then click Save.

4   Choose Window > Workspace > Digital Publishing. Panels that are useful for app authoring are displayed along the right edge of the workspaces, and other panels are collapsed to icons.

▶ **Tip:** You can also change the workspace by clicking the Workspace menu near the right end of the Application Bar across the top of the monitor.

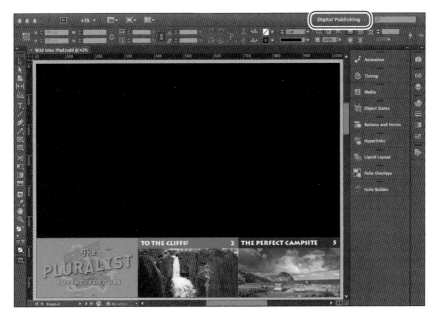

Adding interactive elements

Interactive elements in a digital publication include slide shows, hyperlinks, graphics that a viewer can pan and zoom inside a frame, movies, and sounds. Much like you can modify a graphics frame by adding a stroke or a special effect like a drop shadow or rotation, you can control how interactive elements look and work.

Creating a hyperlink from an object

You'll create a hyperlink from a navigation screen to an article in the document. Before you do that, first take a quick look at the pages in the document that will make up the iPad app.

1   Click the Next Page button to view each of the six pages in the document in turn. The first page is the startup screen for the app; the second page is a navigation screen with a blank space at the top for an introductory video and a directory to two sections in the app that contain stories ("To The Cliffs!" and "The Perfect Campsite"). Only the first story is included in the sample document used in this lesson.

2   Navigate to page Front-2, the second page in the document.

3   With the Selection tool ( ) (V), select the To The Cliffs! object. This is a group containing photo, graphic, and text elements.

Tip: If you want to add new interactive elements, such as buttons, that aren't already on the layout, you can use predefined objects that are included with InDesign. Choose Sample Buttons and Forms from the Buttons and Forms panel menu.

4   Open the Hyperlinks panel. It should be visible in the stack of docked panels along the right side of the monitor as part of the Digital Publishing workspace.

5   Click the Create New Hyperlink button.

6   In the New Hyperlink dialog box, set the following options:

- For Link To, make sure Page is selected. Notice that the Link To menu lets you set up hyperlinks to other types of destinations, such as a URL, email address, or file.

- For Document, make sure Wild Isles iPad.indd (the current document) is selected.

- For Page, choose Main-1.

- Leave the Type set to Invisible Rectangle and leave Highlight set to None.

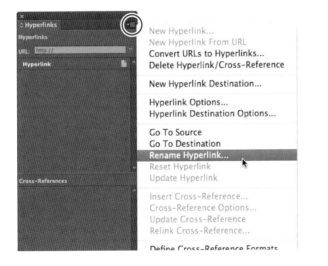

7   Click OK to close the New Hyperlink dialog box.

8   Choose Rename Hyperlink from the Hyperlink panel menu, enter **Banyan Cliffs**, and click OK.

9   Choose File > Save.

Comparing buttons and hyperlinks

You can use buttons and hyperlinks to build navigation controls in InDesign. At first glance, it might seem that there's overlap between what buttons and hyperlinks can do, so to choose between them, you need to know a few key differences in how they work.

Buttons are generally graphic in nature, such as a picture or drawn object that you set up as a button. A button works much like a graphics frame; for example, you can replace the contents of a button. Buttons can also have multiple states. Options for buttons are in the Buttons panel (Window > Interactive > Buttons and Forms). You're more likely to use buttons in graphically engaging multimedia projects where appearance and compelling interactivity is important.

Although you can create a hyperlink from a graphic, hyperlinks are generally text-based and can be generated from text. For example, InDesign can create a live URL hyperlink from URL text you've selected. Hyperlinks have fewer display and rollover options than buttons, and have only a couple of basic states. Hyperlink options are in the Hyperlinks panel (Window > Interactive > Hyperlinks). You're more likely to use hyperlinks in a text-heavy reference document where the hyperlinks may be automatically generated and also automatically preserved when you export the file to an EPUB or PDF.

You can test the hyperlink using the Hyperlinks panel.

1   Make sure the To The Cliffs! object is selected.

▶ **Tip:** To add an interactive element that's available on every page, place it on a master page.

2   In the Hyperlinks panel, make sure the Banyan Cliffs hyperlink is selected. Then click the Go To Destination button to navigate to page Main-1, the first page of the "Journey to Banyan Cliffs" article.

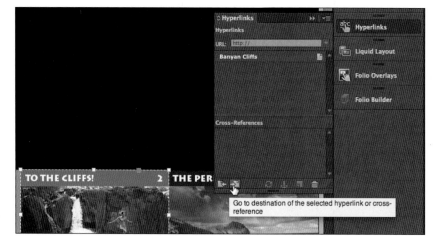

3 In the Hyperlinks panel, make sure the Banyan Cliffs hyperlink is selected and click the Go To Source button. This brings you back to the object that will lead to that destination when tapped on an iPad.

Adding a video

The large black rectangle on the second page is intended to play a video file, so you'll add that now. The video will play on desktop and mobile devices that support video. Adding a movie to a digital publishing document is the same as adding a photo or illustration to a print document. You'll import a movie into the document and use the Media panel to choose a graphic as the poster image for the movie. Then you'll use the Folio Overlays panel to control how the movie plays.

1 Click the Media panel to open it (or choose Window > Interactive > Media). You use this panel to configure how the video is presented on the page and how it plays.

2 Click the Place a Video or Audio File icon at the bottom-right corner of the Media panel, navigate to the Lesson05 folder, select the My Pluralist Video.mp4 video file that you created in Lesson 5, and click Open.

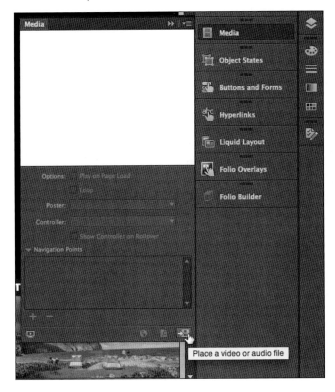

Tip: Clicking the Place a Video or Audio File icon is similar to choosing File > Place.

The video you created in Lesson 5 will play easily on recent iPads because you chose a preset that exported the video at a format and resolution that the iPad handles easily: H.264 format at 1080p HD resolution.

3 Click the loaded Place icon on the black rectangle. It may take a moment for InDesign to finish importing the video.

4 With the rectangle selected, choose Object > Fitting > Fit Content Proportionally to ensure that the video is scaled to fit within the frame.

5 In the Media panel, click the play button to play the video once from beginning to end. Playback occurs in the Media panel but not in the layout; you'll preview layout playback later.

6 In the Media panel, click the Poster menu and choose From Current Frame. The poster frame is a still image that represents the video when the video isn't playing.

7 Drag the time slider to approximately 6 seconds. If the rectangle on the layout doesn't automatically update the poster frame from the time you just set, click the refresh button ().

You might have noticed that there were other video control options in the Media panel that were not changed. Many of those options apply to interactivity when you plan to export to PDF or SWF. For an iPad app, you'll control options in the Folio Options panel. A *folio* is an intermediate document type that you use for building tablet and smartphone apps with Digital Publishing Suite.

App Store apps versus iBooks documents

The ability to submit unlimited iPad apps using Adobe Creative Cloud is intended for interactive media works that could be submitted to the Apple App Store, such as the app you create in this lesson, which mixes hyperlinked elements of an online store and multimedia with graphics and text. If you intend to distribute a work that is only text and graphics with minimal interactivity, that type of document may be regarded as falling within the scope of iBooks, not within the scope of the App Store. Before you begin designing an iPad app for App Store distribution, be sure to review the Apple App Store content submission guidelines to help ensure that your app submission is accepted.

1 Close the Media panel and open the Folio Overlays panel (Window > Folio Overlays).

2 For Video, select Auto Play to play the video when its page is opened, and select Tap to View Controller so that tapping the video on a tablet will display the video controller.

● **Note:** If the Folio Overlays panel doesn't display Audio & Video options, deselect the rectangle containing the video and then select it again.

Naturally, you'll want to preview the interactivity and video you've added so far, so you'll do that next.

Previewing the app on your computer

You don't need to have an iPad to preview how your app works. The Adobe Content Viewer application integrates with InDesign to simulate app behavior on your computer. Adobe Content Viewer was installed when you installed DPS Desktop Tools.

1 At the bottom of the Folio Overlays panel, click Preview and choose Preview on Desktop.

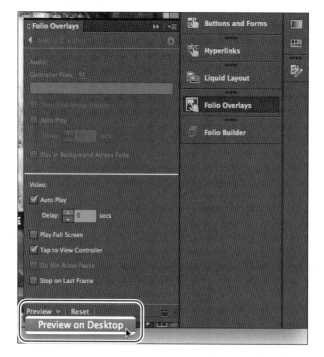

InDesign asks you to wait as it builds a temporary folio and then sends it to Adobe Content Viewer, which starts and displays the folio.

Learn more

DPS Tips by Bob Bringhurst is an iPad app by Adobe that walks you through the process of designing and producing an iPad app, and submitting it to the Apple App Store. It describes many best practices for creating apps with Digital Publishing Suite, Single Edition.

When you're working in DPS App Builder, you can click the Help menu to open the Step-by-step Guide for Single Edition, a PDF file that describes the details of publishing iPad apps with DPS Single Edition, particularly those having to do with developer certificates and other App Store technical requirements for app submissions.

2 View the other pages in the folio by pressing the up arrow key or the down arrow key to simulate swipe gestures on a tablet.

● **Note:** The thin black strip along the right edge of the Content Viewer preview is not a layout error; it's a very narrow scroll bar.

3 Navigate to the second page and click the movie. The movie plays back, and the controller automatically hides after about five seconds.

4 Click the To The Cliffs! text or the picture below it. The app scrolls to the "Journey to Banyan Cliffs" article.

5 Switch back to InDesign.

You'll learn how to preview on an actual iPad later in this lesson.

Adapting to different page sizes with liquid layouts

Tablet applications commonly support viewing in both horizontal and vertical orientations. You can use InDesign to create an iPad app with layouts for both orientations. The app you're creating is currently formatted for a horizontal orientation. Now you'll add another set of pages that are vertically oriented.

You can take advantage of InDesign tools that minimize the amount of time you spend adjusting each page for the rotated layout. For example, Liquid Layout rules determine how an object responds as the size of a layout changes:

- **Scale** simply fills the new page size with the current content resized.

- **Re-center** keeps content centered within the new layout

- **An object-based rule** allows for rules that control a specific object; you can pin any side of an object to maintain its relationship to the edge of a page.

- **A guide-based rule** constrains page adjustment along layout guides you position.

You'll try some of these rules, and then create an alternate layout based on them.

1 In InDesign, open the Liquid Layout panel (Layout > Liquid Layout).

2 On page 1, use the Selection tool to select the orange Pluralist logo near the top-left corner.

3 In the Liquid Layout panel, choose Object-based, and for Pin, select Top and Left. Pin options will maintain the position of the object relative to the top and left page edges, respectively, as the page size changes.

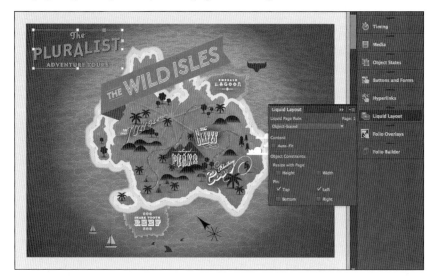

4 With the logo still selected, select the Page tool (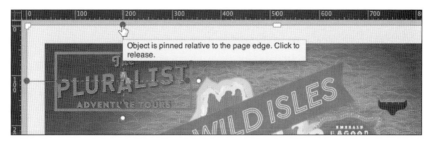) (Shift-P). Notice that when the Page tool is selected, liquid layout handles appear over the selected object (in this case the logo) to indicate how the object will behave when the page is resized. For a more specific description, position the mouse over a handle to read the tool tip that appears.

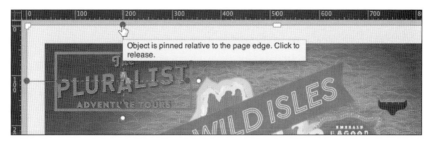

Now you'll test these settings by temporarily changing the page orientation.

5 Select the Page tool. Click the center point in the Reference Point proxy at the left end of the Control panel so that when you change the page orientation, the page will rotate around its center.

6 Click the Portrait orientation icon in the Control panel to see how objects on the page respond to a different orientation. All objects on the page that use Liquid Layout rules should reposition and resize to maintain the intended layout despite the radical change in proportions. Objects not using any rule, such as the Wild Isles map, stay in place as the page rotates around its center.

Note: The border around the map was built in InDesign as four rectangles that are pinned to each of their respective sides of the page using object-based Liquid Layout rules, and allowed to resize to match the page width or height.

Notice that the island graphic fully fills the page vertically. The reason is that the graphic was designed as a square large enough to accommodate both horizontal and vertical orientations. If it had been designed only for the original horizontal layout, there would have been empty space at the top and bottom of the vertical version of the page.

7 Choose Edit > Undo Resize Item to restore the original orientation.

8 Choose File > Save.

You don't have to set layout rules for every object on a page, but every time you're able to apply a rule you reduce the number of objects you need to reposition manually when you create alternate layouts for different screen sizes and orientations.

Creating an alternate vertical layout

InDesign lets you maintain a parallel layout so that you can design for multiple orientations in a single document. This is called creating an alternate layout, and is similar in principle to when you created alternate layouts in Adobe Muse in Chapter 3.

1 Collapse the Liquid Layout panel and open the Pages panel (Window > Pages).

2 Choose Layout > Create Alternate Layout.

3 For Page Size, choose iPad, and make sure the Orientation icon is set to portrait (vertical).

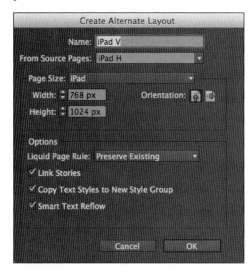

4 Click OK.

In the Pages panel, notice that a new set of pages has appeared in its own column labeled iPad V (as in vertical). In the new alternate layout, all of the original pages were duplicated but using a vertical orientation.

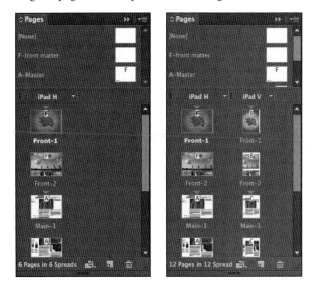

5 In the iPad V layout in the Pages panel, double-click page Front-1, and then view the pages after it.

The first page adapted well to the landscape orientation, but the rest of the pages did not. The reason is that layout rules weren't applied to the rest of the pages. When a layout isn't optimal for layout rules, you can manually recompose the pages, but even here InDesign can save you time using linked content, where content on the alternate layout is dynamically tied to the primary layout. For example, if you have a photo on the primary and alternate layouts and you update the photo on the primary layout, the instance on the alternate layout also updates. This makes it possible for you to manage only one set of content instead of multiple sets, and it's a major reason why it's more convenient to manage layouts for multiple screen sizes using alternate layouts in one InDesign document rather than using multiple documents.

You can resize or reposition the objects that were automatically brought over from the iPad H layout, or you can start over by using the Content Collector to transfer objects from the iPad H layout. For this lesson you'll use the Content Collector to adapt the second page to vertical format. The Content Collector is designed to help you efficiently transfer objects from the primary layouts to alternate layouts.

1 Make sure layout guides are visible. If they aren't, choose View > Grids & Guides > Show Guides.

2 Select the Content Collector tool ( ) (B). The Content Conveyor appears.

3 Select the Content Placer tool ( ), and then select the Create Link option in the Content Conveyor. You can select the Content Placer tool either in the Tools panel (it's grouped with the Content Collector tool) or at the bottom of the Content Conveyor.

   Using the Content Collector is like copying and pasting with the clipboard but gives you more control. For example, you can load items on the Content Collector in a different order than you unload them, and you can make the copies on the alternate layouts linked instances instead of unlinked duplicates.

   Because you'll transfer the objects manually using the Content Collector, you'll delete the objects that were automatically transferred to page Front-2.

4 Go to page Front-2 in the iPad V layout, choose Edit > Select All, and then press the Delete key.

5 Go to page Front-2 in the iPad H layout, and with the Content Collector tool click the video at the top of the page. It's added in the Content Conveyor.

Training with Creative Cloud videos

Having access to the range of Adobe Creative Cloud tools lets you add new skills and capabilities at any time. But being productive with a new tool involves more than just having it; you have to know how to use it. How do you learn all of these new tools? On the Creative Cloud website, the Training section provides videos created by Creative Cloud experts. These materials help you get up to speed on Creative Cloud features, such as iPad app creation.

Simply go to http://creative.adobe.com and sign in with your Adobe ID. Once signed in, click Learn at the top of the Creative Cloud web page. This takes you to a page containing Creative Cloud training videos organized by categories, such as techniques and products. Simply explore the category you want and play the videos that explain the subjects you want to learn.

6   Click the other objects on the page to add them to the Content Conveyor. Pay particular attention to the Pluralist Adventure Video logo because it exists in two parts, the logo and the blue background rectangle; click them separately.

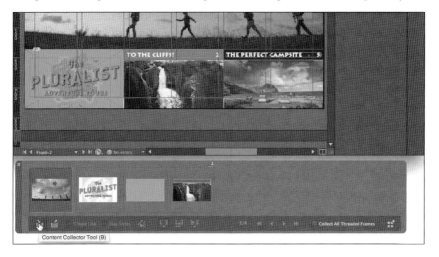

7   Go to page Front-2 in the iPad V layout, and select the Content Placer tool in the Content Conveyor. The pointer changes into a Place icon loaded with every item in the Content Conveyor, starting with the video. (If the thumbnail of the video poster frame is not what's currently loaded, press the left arrow or right arrow key until it is.)

8   Starting from the top-left corner of the page, drag the Content Placer tool down and to the right until the tool snaps to the right edge of the page, so that the rectangle containing the video spans the entire top of the page (reposition and resize if necessary).

▶ **Tip:** You can select the Content Collector and Content Placer tools in both the Tools panel and the Content Conveyor.

9 Choose Object > Fitting > Fit Content to Frame.

● **Note:** If you need to edit an object you've placed, switch to the Selection tool, and then when you're done, switch back to the Content Placer tool to place the remaining objects.

10 With the Content Placer tool selected, press the right arrow key until the To The Cliffs! object is loaded, and drag the pointer down and to the right to add it to the layout. Reposition and resize it until it takes up half the width of the page along the bottom edge. A smart guide will appear when the right edge of the object is exactly halfway across the page.

11 With the Content Placer tool, press the right arrow key until the The Perfect Campsite object is loaded, and drag to add it to the layout. Resize and reposition it as needed until it occupies the right side of the bottom of the page.

12 Load the blue rectangle into the Content Placer tool and add it to the layout. Resize and reposition it as needed until it occupies the remaining free space on the layout.

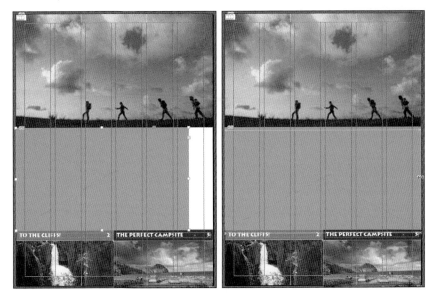

13 Make sure the blue rectangle is deselected (choose Edit > Deselect All if needed), and then drag to add the Pluralist map and text group to the layout, resizing and moving it as needed until it's centered within the blue rectangle.

Now you'll preview the changes you made to the app, but first you'll change the folio preview settings so that InDesign sends both the horizontal and vertical layouts to Adobe Content Viewer.

1   Choose File > Folio Preview Settings, make sure Preview Current Layout is deselected, and click OK.

2   Choose File > Folio Preview. This is the same as clicking Preview at the bottom of the Folio Overlays panel, but can be more convenient when the Folio Overlays panel isn't open.

    InDesign exports the folio to Adobe Content Viewer where you can test the document. Because the folio preview settings were changed to preview all layouts, exporting will take longer than it did previously.

3   Choose commands on the View menu to preview other screen sizes and both orientations. Remember to click the movie you added on page 2 to preview how it plays back.

Publishing your app through a store

To be able to submit an InDesign folio as an app to a store such as the Apple App Store, there are a few more requirements that are outside the scope of this lesson. You'll need:

- An Adobe Digital Publishing Suite account (http://digitalpublishing.acrobat.com), so you can organize, edit, and publish folios with Folio Producer, and arrange articles and edit metadata with Folio Producer Editor. You can sign into Adobe Digital Publishing Suite using your Adobe ID.

- An Adobe Digital Publishing Suite Single Edition serial number to publish a single issue with a single folio, a Professional Edition subscription for unlimited custom viewer apps and folios, or an Enterprise Edition subscription for advanced customization and analytics. You can view pricing information for these options at http://www.adobe.com/products/digital-publishing-suite-family/buying-guide.html.

- Any membership required for the store where you want to submit your app. For example, submitting an app to the Apple App Store requires membership in the Apple iOS Developer Program, which involves an annual fee.

- An Internet connection so that you can interact with Adobe Digital Publishing Suite and the stores where you want to submit your app.

The preceding list does not necessarily cover all of the requirements of publishing an app through a store, so make sure you review and understand the current requirements of the store you want to use as you plan your app. Also, after submitting an app to a store such as the Apple App Store, the app may be subject to examination and approval by that store before it can be distributed.

Creating a folio

A folio is an intermediate file that contains the content of your app, such as the articles that make up each section of your app. Using the Folio Builder panel that's installed into InDesign CC when you install DPS Desktop Tools, you build a folio by importing InDesign CC documents (which become articles), cover/preview images and icons, and any other files locally linked from the InDesign CC documents, such as videos.

You can use the Folio Builder panel to preview folios on your computer using Adobe Content Viewer and also to share folios with others.

Note: When you open the Folio Builder or Folio Overlays panel, you may be asked to sign in with your Adobe ID. Doing so isn't required for this lesson but will be necessary for later stages of iPad app creation that involve the online Folio Producer, Digital Publishing Suite Dashboard, and DPS App Builder (not covered in this lesson).

1   Open the Folio Builder panel (Window > Folio Builder), and click the New Folio button at the bottom of the panel.

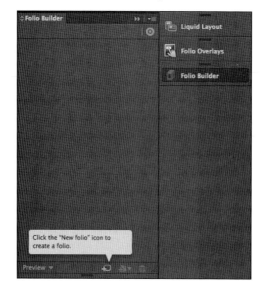

2   In the New Folio dialog box, for Folio Name enter **Pluralist Adventure Tours**.

3   For Target Device select Apple iPad, and click Portrait and Landscape Folio. For Default Format select PDF.

Note: If you are signed in with your Adobe ID, the New Folio dialog box may display an additional option called Create Offline Folio. If it's present, select it for this lesson.

4   Click OK.

5 In the Folio Builder panel, click the Add Article button and choose Add Open InDesign Document.

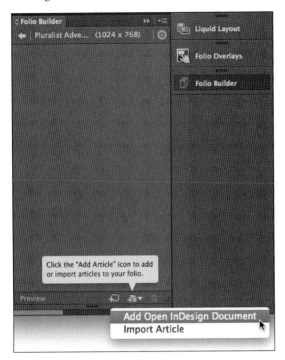

6 In the New Article dialog box, for Article Name enter **Summer Issue**. Notice that your horizontal and vertical InDesign layouts are automatically entered as the Portrait and Landscape layouts for the folio.

7 Click OK. Folio Builder processes the InDesign spreads into a folio document.

When folio creation completes, Summer Issue appears in Folio Builder.

Previewing on an iPad

You've already previewed the iPad app using Adobe Content Viewer on your computer. You can also preview the iPad app by sending its folio to Adobe Content Viewer on an iPad that's connected to your computer with a cable. This lets you test how your app responds to actual use on the iPad, including tablet-specific input such as gestures and orientation changes.

To directly preview folios on the iPad, the iOS version of Adobe Content Viewer (free) must be installed on the iPad. If it isn't installed yet, open the App Store on your iPad, search for Adobe Content Viewer, and install it.

As long as your iPad is properly set up and connected to your computer, InDesign can send folios directly to Adobe Content Viewer on the iPad.

1 Connect the iPad to your computer with the cable you use for syncing the iPad to your computer.

● **Note:** Adobe Content Viewer appears under the name Adobe Viewer on the iOS home screen.

2 On your iPad, start Adobe Viewer.

3 On your computer, in InDesign open the Folio Builder panel (Window > Folio Builder).

4 If the Folio Builder panel is displaying the Summer Issue article of the Pluralist Adventure Tours folio, click the Back to All Folios button. (To preview the entire folio in the next step, the Folio Builder panel must display folios, not articles.)

5 Click Preview and choose Preview on *<the name of your iPad>*. There may be a short delay as the folio receives the preview from InDesign on your computer.

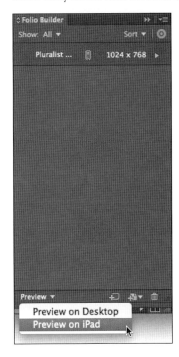

Note: If your iPad is not listed in the Preview button menu, make sure the iPad is connected with a cable that supports synchronizing and make sure Adobe Content Viewer is the active (foreground) app on the iPad; then on your computer restart InDesign and try again.

6 After the folio appears in Adobe Content Viewer, tap to open it. Try navigating pages in both vertical and horizontal orientation.

There is also a way to view folios in Adobe Content Viewer on the iPad without having to connect the iPad with a cable. To do this, both the Folio Builder panel in InDesign and Adobe Content Viewer on the iPad must be logged into your Creative Cloud account with the same Adobe ID. You would then use the Folio Builder panel to upload folios to the Digital Publishing Suite (DPS) website (digitalpublishing. acrobat.com), which is also where you would later move your folios through further production steps on the way to creating an app (see the next section, "Final production steps"). You can then use Adobe Content Viewer on the iPad to view folios stored in your DPS account.

Final production steps

Producing a finished iPad app involves additional production tasks that are not covered in this lesson because they include steps that require you to register as an iOS app developer with Apple. In addition to the folios you produce using InDesign, a finished app must also include:

- Icons for the iPad home screen, in multiple sizes and in PNG format.

- Splash (startup) screen images in both horizontal and vertical orientations and in PNG format. You could use page Cover-1 for this purpose and have the app begin on page Cover-2 instead. In InDesign you can create PNG images from any page by choosing File > Export and selecting PNG as the Format.

- Developer certificates, which are provided by Apple after you register as an iOS app developer.

You would then proceed through the steps for submitting your app to the Apple App Store. You would start by choosing Create App from the Folio Builder panel menu.

DPS App Builder software opens and leads you through the process. You can also use DPS App Builder to manage apps you have submitted.

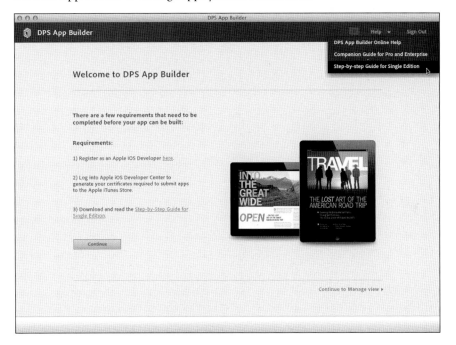

Wrapping up

You've learned how to create an iPad app using InDesign, preview it on your computer, and test it on an actual iPad. You're now ready to start taking advantage of the unlimited number of DPS Single Edition app submissions included with your Creative Cloud subscription by building iPad apps that showcase your work or promote your clients.

Review questions

1 What feature lets you specify how an object maintains a desirable position on an alternate layout that was converted from a primary layout?

2 Why should you use the Content Collector tool, Content Placer tool, and Content Conveyor to copy and paste items between layouts instead of copying and pasting?

3 In InDesign, what is the difference between a button and a hyperlink?

4 What is the intermediate format that's required when creating an iPad app from an InDesign document?

5 What are two ways to preview a folio?

Review answers

1 An object-based page rule lets you control how an object responds to a change in page dimensions. For example, you can pin the top and left edges of a graphic to the page so that it remains at the top-left corner of the page.

2 The Content Collector tool, Content Placer tool, and Content Conveyor let you place and resize objects on a new layout in any order, and you can create linked instances of content that updates with the same content on the original layout.

3 Buttons tend to be graphics and can have multiple visual states, whereas hyperlinks are usually text-based.

4 An InDesign document must be converted into a folio before being converted to an iPad app.

5 You can preview a folio in Adobe Content Viewer on your computer or in Adobe Content Viewer on an iPad connected to your computer.

7 CREATING AN EBOOK

Lesson overview

In this lesson you'll learn essential skills and techniques that will help you convert a printed brochure to a mobile format:

- Understanding the limitations of the EPUB format for eBooks
- Preparing InDesign CC text and graphics for an eBook layout
- Exporting to the EPUB format

You'll probably need less than one hour to complete this lesson. Download the project files for this lesson from the Lesson & Update Files tab on your Account page at www.peachpit.com and store them on your computer in a convenient location, as described in the "Getting Started" section of this book. Your Accounts page is also where you'll find any updates to the chapters or to the lesson files. Look on the Lesson & Update Files tab to access the most current content.

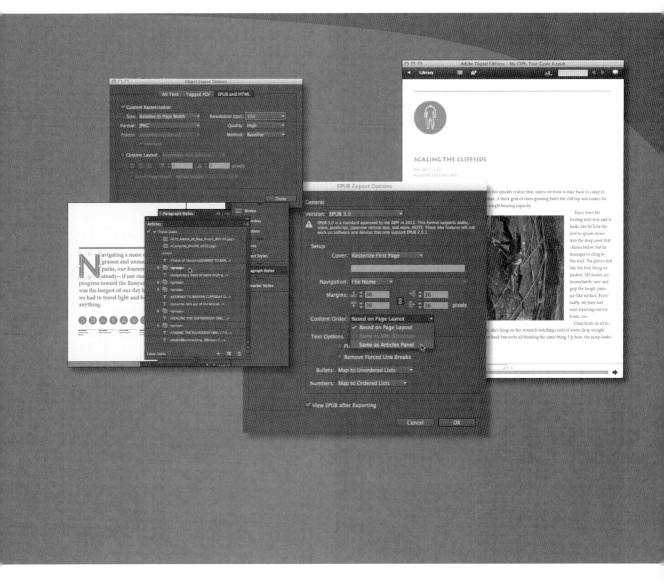

Learn about the special requirements of producing an
eBook in the EPUB format and how to create an EPUB
eBook using Adobe InDesign CC.

Note: If you have not already downloaded the project files for this lesson to your computer from your Account page, make sure you do so now. See "Getting Started" at the beginning of the book.

Setting up to create an eBook

In this lesson, you'll put the finishing touches on a promotional booklet, export the document as an eBook in the EPUB format, and then preview the exported document.

The EPUB standard was designed to let publishers create reflowable content that can be displayed on a wide variety of electronic reading devices. You can read EPUB documents using products such as the Barnes & Noble Nook, Kobo eReader, Apple iBooks for iPad, iPhone, Sony Reader, and Adobe Digital Editions software that runs on Mac and Windows computers.

The size of e-reader screens varies from device to device, readers have some control over the size of displayed text, and content flows in a single continuous thread. For these reasons, the page size of the InDesign document doesn't have to correspond to any particular screen size. In general, graphics should be sized to fit within the typical column width of an EPUB reader; be aware that some devices or readers may display two or more columns when the device screen or the window of the EPUB reader software has a wide aspect ratio.

EPUB is primarily intended for a single text story, such as the chapter of a novel or textbook with occasional illustrations. The current EPUB format does not easily accommodate heavily designed layouts and doesn't support design techniques such as overlapping objects or advanced typography. When you want to export a design-oriented document to the EPUB format, you'll need to export each creatively composed layout in the sample publication as a single rasterized image. When you want to create a digital publication in which sophisticated page designs must be preserved, consider creating a tablet application with the Digital Publishing Suite, as you did in Chapter 6.

Installing Adobe Digital Editions

To be able to read the EPUB format documents you'll produce during this lesson on your computer, Adobe Digital Editions software must be installed on your computer. You can use Adobe Digital Editions software to download eBooks and other digital content, and read them both online and offline. You can also highlight text and add comments, as well as borrow eBooks from libraries.

1   Using your web browser, go to www.adobe.com/products/digitaleditions.

2   On the web page, scroll down to Getting Started and click the Download Adobe Digital Editions link.

3   Download the version for your operating system, open and run the installer, and follow the installation instructions.

Viewing the sample document as an eBook

In this lesson, you'll convert the same print-oriented InDesign document to more than one output format. So that you can easily start from scratch for each part of the lesson, the sample InDesign document is saved as a template.

1 Start InDesign CC. To ensure that the panels and menu commands match those used in this lesson, choose Window > Workspace > Advanced, and then choose Window > Workspace > Reset Advanced. To begin working, you'll open an InDesign document that is already partially adapted for an EPUB export.

2 Open the Lesson07 folder in your Lessons folder, and double-click the file Cliffs Tour Guide.indt. Navigate through the pages in the document to see how it's currently laid out.

3 Choose File > Save As, and save the document into your Lesson07 folder as **My Cliffs Tour Guide.indd**. If you find the guides distracting, press W to switch to Document Preview mode.

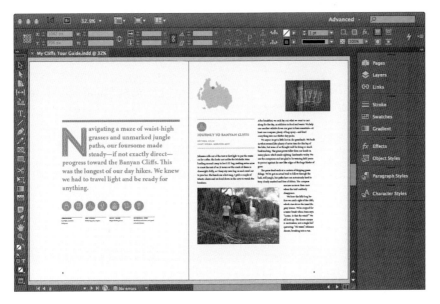

You can see that this is a print-oriented document with multiple-column layouts. The EPUB format is not set up to accommodate the level of design in this document. You'll export an EPUB version of the current document to observe this.

4 Choose File > Export. Navigate into the EPUB Exported folder in your Lesson07 folder, choose EPUB from the Format menu, name it **My Cliffs Tour Guide 1.epub**, and click Save.

5 In the EPUB Export Options dialog box, make sure View EPUB After Exporting is selected, leave the rest of the options at their default settings, and click OK. The EPUB document opens in Adobe Digital Editions.

EPUB Export Options

General
Image
Advanced

General

Version: EPUB 3.0

⚠ EPUB 3.0 is a standard approved by the IDPF in 2011. This format supports audio, video, JavaScript, Japanese vertical text, and more. NOTE: These new features will not work on software and devices that only support EPUB 2.0.1.

Setup

Cover: Rasterize First Page

Navigation: File Name

Margins: 0   0
0   0   pixels

Content Order: Based on Page Layout

Text Options

☐ Place Footnote After Paragraph
☐ Remove Forced Line Breaks

Bullets: Map to Unordered Lists

Numbers: Map to Ordered Lists

☑ View EPUB after Exporting

Cancel   OK

6 Scroll through the document using the scroll bar, the left arrow and right arrow keys, or the Page Up and Page Down keys.

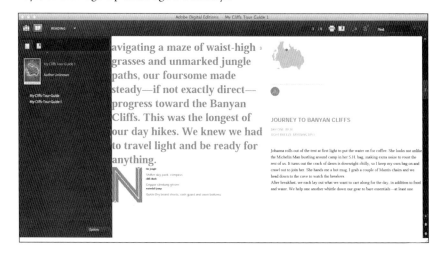

The appearance of the EPUB version is likely to be disappointing. The formerly composed objects and images appear in a one-column sequence of objects, and some objects are in the wrong order. The multiple columns of text are now a single column. Also, the margins are too small. Overall, the design seems to have disintegrated. You'll soon resolve all of these problems.

Tip: If the EPUB opens in an application other than Adobe Digital Editions, close that application. Then start Adobe Digital Editions and click the All Items bookshelf, switch to the desktop and locate the EPUB file you exported in step 4, and drag that file into the Adobe Digital Editions window.

7   Return to InDesign and choose File > Save.

Preparing a publication for an EPUB export

Getting an InDesign document ready for an EPUB export generally involves several major stages:

• Map text styles to CSS styles.

• Arrange page objects in the proper sequence for a single flow of text and graphics using the Articles panel.

• Rasterize complex page layouts into images.

You'll complete each stage separately, and you'll use Adobe Digital Editions to preview the state of the EPUB version as you go through the process.

Mapping text styles to CSS

The EPUB format is a variation on CSS styles and HTML markup, which are in turn related to XML (Extensible Markup Language). When you use paragraph styles, InDesign can translate much of the text formatting you apply in InDesign into CSS.

1   In InDesign, go to page 9, and with the Type tool click an insertion point in the Journey to Banyan Cliffs text.

2   Open the Paragraph Styles panel (Window > Styles > Paragraph Styles), and double-click the Subhead A style.

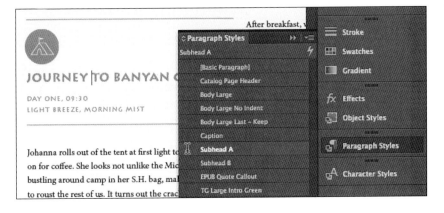

3 In the Paragraph Style Options dialog box, click Export Tagging.

The Export Tagging section lets you map InDesign styles to tags you use when exporting to EPUB, HTML, or PDF to better preserve the structure and presentation of your document. By default, the Tag menu is set to Automatic, but if your project requires specific style mappings, you can choose them here.

In the Export Details section, you can see how InDesign will translate the tag upon export. In this case, the Subhead A style is currently set to automatically map to the p (paragraph) tag. Instead, you'll manually map Subhead A to a heading style because Subhead A is not paragraph body text.

▶ **Tip:** The Split EPUB option you see in the Edit All Export Tags dialog box provides a way to insert a page break before specific paragraph styles. You may want to do this to control pagination and make long documents easier to navigate. However, this option results in a higher number of files in the EPUB package.

4 In the EPUB and HTML section, click the Tag menu and choose h1. You'll see that the Tag readout in Export Details updates to show the change you made.

Mapping Subhead A to h1 will not necessarily result in a visual change to the EPUB, although it may if a custom Cascading Style Sheet document is attached or depending on how a specific EPUB reader displays text.

5 Click OK and save the document.

Online publishing with the EPUB format

The rise of eBook readers brought about the need for a standard format optimized for onscreen reading. A format that performs this role is EPUB, a digital version of a conventional printed book. The EPUB format is an open eBook standard. EPUB files can be read on a diverse range of eBook readers—from handheld devices (like the Sony Reader and Barnes & Noble Nook) to reading applications for desktops, tablets, and smartphones. EPUB documents can be converted into other formats, such as the MOBI format compatible with the Amazon Kindle.

EPUB is an XML-based format designed to enable text to reflow according to the capabilities of various eBook readers, which means that you can resize the text, change the font, or view an eBook on different screen sizes, and the text will reflow to fill the available view area. This makes the EPUB format the best choice for eBooks that are read on small handheld reading devices. In contrast, the PDF format preserves the original layout of a document, giving you complete control over page design and presentation. PDF is the optimal choice for eBooks that have a complex design or will only be read on regular-sized computer screens.

The EPUB format does not define page structure, so content flows as one continuous, linear stream similar to a word processor document. If your layout is simple, conversion to the EPUB format may be relatively straightforward. However, design-intensive publications may require manual intervention to appear in a readable sequence in an EPUB file.

InDesign provides tools, such as the Articles panel, which help you adapt documents to the EPUB format. You can then export directly from InDesign to the EPUB format. To preview your EPUB documents, use Adobe Digital Editions software, which is a free download from adobe.com.

Arranging objects into a single-column flow

As you scrolled through the initial export, you probably noticed a great deal of visual clutter in the conversion. In addition, some objects are in a different order because of ambiguity in translating a freely designed two-dimensional layout to a single column in the EPUB format. You'll now clean up many of these display issues by eliminating some unneeded objects from the EPUB export and specifically setting the object sequence for the EPUB version by using the articles feature.

In InDesign, an article is a way to organize content for digital publishing. You can use articles to specify which page objects are included in the digital version of a publication and also to control the sequence in which those objects appear. Controlling the sequence is especially important in formats that support only a one-column stream of content such as EPUB. You'll use the Articles panel, which is tailor-made for these tasks. An article has already been created in this document; you'll learn how to add objects to it.

1　In InDesign, open the Articles panel (Window > Articles).

2　Click the disclosure triangle next to the Travel Guide article to expand it and reveal its contents. The Travel Guide article already contains some of the objects in the document.

3　In the Articles panel, double-click the first item in the Travel Guide article. InDesign jumps to the cover (a single graphic imported from Adobe Illustrator CC) and selects it.

4　Double-click each of the next few items in the article to see the objects they represent. Notice which icons in the Articles panel represent graphics, text frames, groups, lines, and paths.

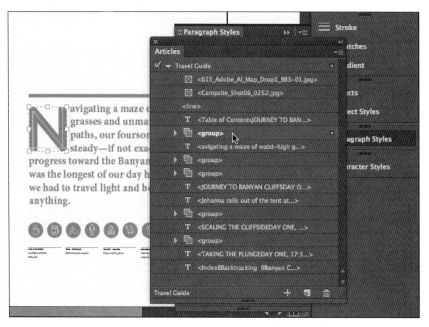

If you scroll through the EPUB document exported earlier that's open in Adobe Digital Editions, you'll see that a drop cap is out of sequence; it appears at the end of the paragraph it's supposed to introduce. But in InDesign, as you double-click the objects in the Articles panel, you can observe that the drop cap is in the correct sequence there.

Also notice that there were a few items on the InDesign layout that are not listed in the Articles panel but appear in the exported EPUB, such as the Table of Contents on page 3 and the backpacks on page 11. The designer of this document intended to exclude those objects from the EPUB. You'll now set an option in the EPUB Export Options dialog box that will allow the Articles panel to dictate the flow of EPUB content.

5　Choose File > Export. Navigate into the EPUB Exported folder in your Lesson07 folder, choose EPUB from the Format menu, name it **My Cliffs Tour Guide 2.epub**, and click Save.

Now that you're back in the EPUB Export Options dialog box, this is a great time to increase the margins to give the EPUB layout a little more breathing room.

6　Enter **36** in the first Margins option (the top margin), and then press the Tab key. All of the Margins fields should update when you press Tab. If they don't, click the link icon to select it so that all the values change when you edit any one of them.

In the General pane of the EPUB Export Options dialog box, notice that the Content Order menu is set to Based on Page Layout. You'll change this setting next.

7　Click the Content Order menu and choose Same as Articles Panel.

8 Click OK. InDesign exports the new EPUB document and opens it in Adobe Digital Editions.

If you compare this version (its filename ends in 2) with the previous version you exported, you'll see that the layout is cleaner. Distracting loose elements have been suppressed and the sequence is now correct (both due to the control of the Articles panel). In addition, the margins have increased, resulting in a more attractive layout.

However, there are still some display issues. For example, the drop cap after the Table of Contents is no longer aligned with its paragraph. You'll address this next.

Rasterizing page layouts and working with the Articles panel

To preserve highly graphical layouts in the EPUB format, you can set them up to be rasterized at export time. Any pages that primarily consist of imported and graphic objects must be grouped into a single object and then set up for rasterization. In this example, you'll rasterize the teal introductory paragraph because the drop cap, rules, oversized type, and icons make it too typographically complex for the EPUB format.

You'll first group the objects that need to stay together and set them up in the Articles panel as a unit. The Articles panel can contain more than one instance of each object, so after you add the new group to the Articles panel, you'll need to remove the old, ungrouped instances of the same objects.

1 In InDesign, go to page 8, and with the Selection tool drag a selection marquee around all of the objects on page 8 except the gray rules and text at the bottom.

2 With the objects selected, choose Object > Group.

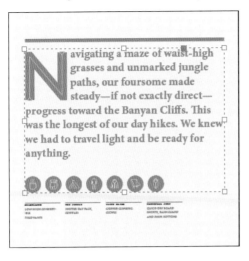

3 With the group selected, choose Object > Object Export Options.

4 In the Object Export Options dialog box, click the EPUB and HTML tab, and select Custom Rasterization. For Resolution (ppi), choose 150. Leave the other settings as they are, and click Done.

▶ **Tip:** You can include Custom Rasterization settings in an object style so that they are easy to apply to and modify many objects or groups.

Because the EPUB settings use the Articles panel to describe the sequence of objects in the EPUB version, you need to remove the old ungrouped objects from the Articles panel and add the new group to the panel in the correct position in the sequence.

1 In the Articles panel, double-click the first item named <group>. This represents just the N drop cap that was in the Articles panel before you added the new group.

2   Shift-click the subsequent two objects in the Articles panel so that all three are selected. Then click the Delete button in the Articles panel to remove the old, ungrouped instances of the drop cap, the paragraph, and the row of icons.

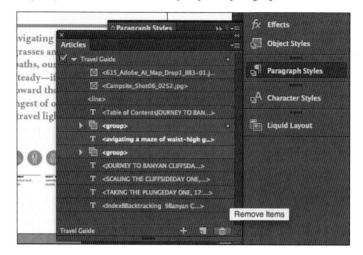

3   With the Selection tool, click the entire group containing the drop cap on the layout, and in the Articles panel, select the Travel Guide article; then click the Add Selection to Articles button. The group is added at the bottom of the Travel Guide article.

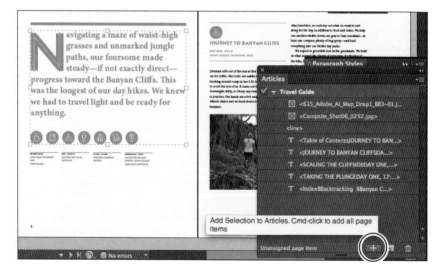

4 In the Articles panel, drag the new group up so that it appears after Table of Contents in the list.

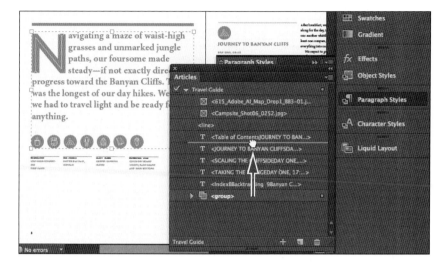

5 To verify the list of objects that the article includes for EPUB export, double-click the Table of Contents object item and the two groups that follow it in the Articles panel. The objects selected should include the Table of Contents, the entire group containing the drop cap, the paragraph, and icons, as well as the continent graphic. This list represents the sequence of objects that will be displayed within the article in the EPUB document.

Now you'll export another test version to see the effect of the changes you've made so far.

1 Choose File > Export. Navigate into the EPUB Exported folder in your Lesson07 folder, choose EPUB from the Format menu, name it **My Cliffs Tour Guide 3.epub**, and click Save.

In the EPUB Export Options dialog box that appears, notice that there is a Cover option and that it's set at Rasterize First Page. Because many eBooks primarily consist of text but have a highly visual cover design, this option makes it possible to rasterize the cover at export time so you don't have to manually group and rasterize it.

2 Make sure View EPUB After Exporting is selected, leave the rest of the options at their default settings, and click OK. The EPUB document opens in Adobe Digital Editions.

3 In Adobe Digital Editions, scroll until you see the group you just worked on. The good news is that the design of that group has been preserved, but the smoothness of the type may not be ideal at all sizes because it was converted to an image. In addition, there are still some problems with page breaks.

4 Return to InDesign and save the document.

Although rasterization is a reasonable option to preserve a design in the EPUB format, it's important not to become too reliant on this method. The reason is that when content containing text is converted into an image, it becomes nonsearchable, pagination becomes more difficult, and the document's file size increases dramatically.

Applying object styles for EPUB documents

In the EPUB version in Adobe Digital Editions, section headings often start and break in awkward places. The headings begin with graphics, so one way to address page breaks is to create an object style that always creates a page break before the object.

1 With the Selection tool, select the drop cap group you created on page 8.

2 In the Objects Styles panel (Window > Styles > Object Styles), Alt-click/Option-click the Create New Style icon.

3 In the New Object Style dialog box, enter **Break Graphic** for the Style Name.

4 Select the Apply Style to Selection option and the Preview option at the bottom left of the dialog box. The appearance of the selected group may change, but don't be concerned about that at the moment.

5 In the Basic Attributes section and Effects section, click any check marks to change them to dashes. Leave empty check boxes as they are. Don't alter check marks in the Export Options section, because this style is designed to apply changes in that section.

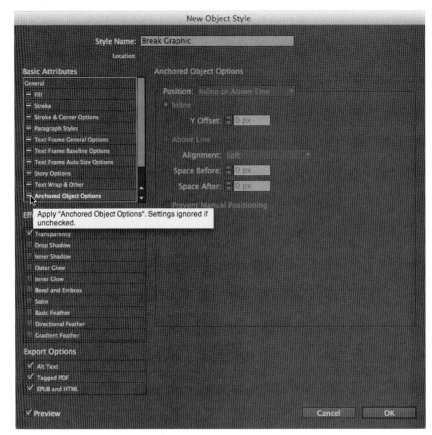

A check mark means that the style will alter that option for the selected object, whereas a dash means the style will leave the selected object's setting unchanged for that option. As you change the check marks to dashes, the original settings of the group are restored.

6 In the Export Options section, select EPUB and HTML (click the text, not the check box).

7 In the EPUB and HTML section, make sure Custom Rasterization is selected with Resolution set to 150ppi.

8 Select Custom Layout, click the Custom Layout menu, and then choose Alignment and Spacing.

9 Select Insert Page Break, click the Insert Page Break menu, and then choose Before Image.

10 Click OK to close the New Object Style dialog box.

11 On page 9, use the Selection tool to select the Australia continent silhouette, and in the Object Styles panel, click Break Graphic.

12 Repeat step 11 to apply the Break Graphic object style to the "Half a mile out…" text frame on page 10.

13 Repeat step 11 to apply the Break Graphic object style to the graphic above the "Taking the plunge" text on page 11.

Adding metadata

When an EPUB document is listed in an e-reader or other database, the information that's visible is taken from the metadata for the file. It's a good idea to customize that information.

1 Choose File > File Info.

▶ **Tip:** When you're applying an object style, always select an object with the Selection tool. You can apply an object style only to frames you selected with the Selection tool, not to text you highlighted with the Type tool.

2 For Document Title, type **Cliffs Tour Guide**. For Author, type your name.

Note that the rest of the dialog box gives you an opportunity to enter detailed descriptive text, including a copyright notice.

3 Click OK.

Previewing the final version

Now it's time to export the document again to see whether the settings you changed will result in a better EPUB document than the one you exported earlier.

You'll export another test version to see the effect of the changes you've made.

1 Choose File > Export. Navigate into the EPUB Exported folder in your Lesson07 folder, choose EPUB from the Format menu, name it **My Cliffs Tour Guide 4.epub**, and click Save.

Although many of the EPUB export options can remain at their default settings, consider adjusting the following options:

- If your document uses bulleted or numbered lists, in the Text Options section in the General pane, it's a good idea to choose Map to Unordered Lists in the Bullets menu and choose Map to Ordered Lists in the Numbers menu.

- In the Image pane, make sure Preserve Appearance from Layout is selected to maintain image cropping and settings.

Note: Although InDesign can embed fonts in EPUB documents, not all e-readers support font embedding. If possible, test your EPUB on various devices to ensure that you're satisfied with the output.

Tip: It's a good idea to test your EPUB document on as many smartphones, tablets, and computer-based EPUB reader applications as possible. Use Creative Cloud file synchronization or other online sharing services to copy the files to other devices.

- In the Advanced pane, leave all the check boxes selected to help preserve the original appearance of the document.

Note: InDesign automatically generates a Unique ID for an EPUB; however, for commercial EPUBs, you would enter the eBook's ISBN instead.

2 Make sure View EPUB After Exporting is selected, leave the rest of the options at their default settings, and click OK. The EPUB document opens in Adobe Digital Editions.

The result this time should look much better, resolving the issues you saw in the previous version you exported to EPUB. If you were to design an EPUB document from scratch, you would design it as one long text story with full-page layouts consolidated into single, rasterized graphics.

The Table of Contents near the beginning of the document and the Index at the end of the document were both generated automatically by the table of contents and indexing features in InDesign, and preserved during an EPUB export. They are both interactive, so you can click Table of Contents entries or Index page numbers to jump directly to their referenced content.

3 Exit Adobe Digital Editions. Switch to InDesign, save the document, and exit InDesign.

Wrapping up

You've learned how to create an EPUB document using InDesign and preview it in Adobe Digital Editions, opening up the possibility of publishing to a wide variety of EPUB-compatible reading devices and software on computers, tablets, and smartphones.

Review questions

1 When is it preferable to export a digital publication in the EPUB format?

2 What aspects of a print-oriented layout can create additional work when converting to EPUB format?

3 What are three key steps in preparing most publications for export to the EPUB format?

4 What are two reasons you would use the Articles panel to help create an EPUB document?

5 You want to keep some graphics-oriented content as a unit so they don't break up during an EPUB export. How should you do this?

Review answers

1 Use the EPUB format when you want your document to be available on a very wide range of mobile devices and by many eBook reader applications on computers.

2 Print layouts may contain multiple columns, overlapping objects, and advanced typography. Those layout features are not directly supported in the EPUB format, but features in InDesign let you adapt print layouts for a successful EPUB conversion.

3 You should consider mapping text styles to CSS, arranging objects for a single-column presentation using the Articles panel, and rasterizing complex page layouts.

4 The Articles panel helps sequence page objects for a single-column text flow and lets you specify which objects should be included in an EPUB export (suppressing the rest).

5 To keep graphics-oriented content as a unit when exporting to an EPUB document, rasterize them into a single image.

8 CREATING INTERACTIVE FORMS

Lesson overview

In this lesson you'll learn how to create PDF forms by using form tools in Adobe InDesign. You'll learn these skills and techniques:

- Quickly laying out a form using a table grid

- Adding different types of form objects, such as text fields, radio buttons, check boxes, and combo boxes

- Duplicating form objects

- Testing your form in Adobe Acrobat Pro

 You'll probably need about an hour to complete this lesson. Download the project files for this lesson from the Lesson & Update Files tab on your Account page at www.peachpit.com and store them on your computer in a convenient location, as described in the "Getting Started" section of this book. Your Accounts page is also where you'll find any updates to the chapters or to the lesson files. Look on the Lesson & Update Files tab to access the most current content.

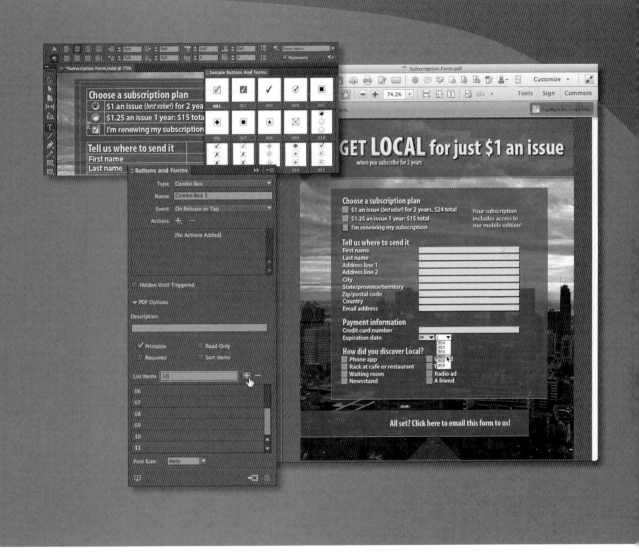

Learn how to combine advanced layout and typography tools with powerful form tools in Adobe InDesign CC to produce PDF forms that are easy to fill out.

Note: If you have not already downloaded the project files for this lesson to your computer from your Account page, make sure you do so now. See "Getting Started" at the beginning of the book.

Creating PDF forms in Adobe InDesign

Adobe InDesign CC includes form-building tools that you can use together with its advanced layout and typography features to create PDF forms that are functional and well designed. It was still possible to design a form in earlier versions of InDesign (before InDesign CS6), but the actual form elements had to be added in Adobe Acrobat Pro XI. Now you can accomplish most form-building tasks in InDesign CC alone, although you'll still check your work in Acrobat Pro.

The decisions you make with the form tools should be based on the data formats required for your data to be processed correctly by the database that will receive it. Before you begin designing an interactive form, discuss your goals with your web developers and have them review the design, the form field values, and any code or scripts used in the form. They might suggest ways to set up your form so that it collects your data efficiently and integrates smoothly with the receiving database. Fortunately, you don't need to be connected to a server or a database to design a form using InDesign.

Getting started

In this lesson you'll develop a subscription form for the magazine you worked with in Chapter 2. The form is already partially built, and it's saved as a template file in your Lesson08 folder. You'll open it and take a look at how it's been put together so far.

1 In Adobe Bridge CC, navigate to the Lesson08 folder in your Lessons folder.

2 Double-click the file Subscription Form.indt to open it in InDesign CC.

3 Choose View > Fit Page in Window. The partially built form is in the large rectangle in the middle of the page. The form structure may not be visible if the document opened in the Preview screen mode.

4 Choose File > Save As, enter the filename **Subscription Form.indd,** navigate to your Lesson08 folder, and click Save.

5 Choose Interactive for PDF from the workspace menu near the right side of the Application Bar, or choose Window > Workspace > Interactive for PDF. This applies the Interactive for PDF workspace, which displays the panels you're likely to use for projects that result in a PDF file with interactive elements, such as this form.

6 Choose View > Screen Mode and make sure Normal is selected, or press the W key to toggle the screen mode to Normal. In Normal screen mode, the text frames and table grid are visible. Although you can edit in Preview mode, you'll probably find it easier to work in Normal mode where object outlines are visible.

Preview screen mode   Normal screen mode

7 Zoom in so that you can see the top of the form more clearly.

To make it easy to align form objects with their labels, this form is laid out using a table. You'll paste form objects into it as inline graphics so they flow with the table. You can also lay out forms using text with tabs or even as individual text and form objects that you select and line up using the Align panel. The simplest way to develop the form used in this lesson was to use a table.

Using the Sample Buttons and Forms panel

Next, you'll add radio buttons and check boxes to the form.

1 Choose Window > Interactive > Buttons and Forms.

You use this panel to control how a form object works, but the options in the panel are available only when a form object is selected. There aren't any form objects in this document yet, only the layout and text for the form, so you'll add some form objects now. Fortunately, instead of having to design them from scratch, you can use premade form objects.

2 Choose Sample Buttons And Forms from the Button and Forms panel menu, and then scroll the panel to examine the form objects that are available.

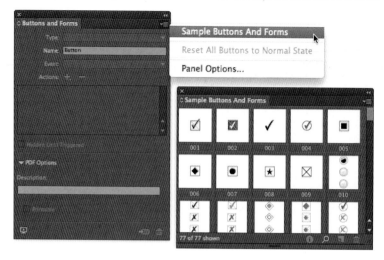

The Sample Buttons and Forms panel is an InDesign library that contains a range of check boxes, radio buttons, and buttons of various shapes and designs.

● **Note:** When a form object, such as a button, radio button, or check box, is selected on the layout, you may see multiple states listed in the Buttons and Forms panel. These provide alternate appearances of a form object, which indicate when it's selected or not selected, or when the mouse pointer is over it.

3 In the Sample Buttons and Forms panel, drag the radio button set 017 to the left of the heading for the first group of options in "Choose a subscription plan." The exact position doesn't matter right now.

● **Note:** There are two different Constrain Proportions (link) icons near each other in the Control panel, so make sure you click the correct one, as shown in the figure for step 4.

4 With the three radio buttons still selected, make sure the "Constrain proportions for width & height" button is selected in the Control panel, enter **1p2** into the W (Width) field in the Control panel, and press Enter/Return.

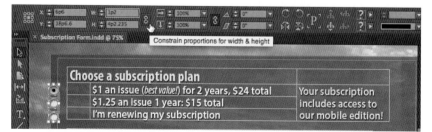

5 Choose Edit > Deselect All.

6 With the Selection tool (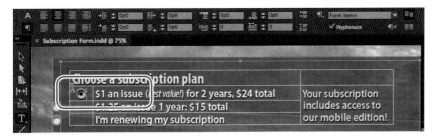), select the first radio button and choose Edit > Cut.

7 With the Type tool ( ), click an insertion point in the table cell to the left of the label "$1 an issue…" and choose Edit > Paste.

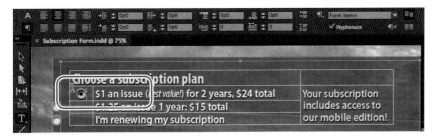

8 Repeat step 6 for the second radio button, pasting it into the table cell below the first radio button.

The third choice, "I'm renewing my subscription," is actually independent of the first two. You'll replace it with a check box so that the person filling out the form can first select a subscription plan and then specify whether it is a renewal.

9 With the Selection tool, select the third radio button and press the Delete key.

10 In the Sample Buttons and Forms panel, drag the check box 001 to the left of the two radio buttons; again, the exact placement isn't critical.

11 With the check box still selected, make sure the "Constrain proportions for width & height" button is selected in the Control panel, enter **1p2** into the W (Width) field in the Control panel, and press Enter/Return.

12 With the Selection tool, select the check box and choose Edit > Cut.

13 With the Type tool, click an insertion point in the table cell to the left of the label "I'm renewing…" and choose Edit > Paste.

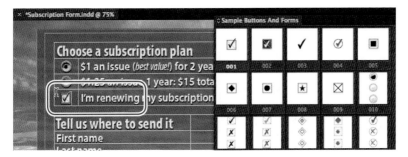

14 Choose Edit > Deselect All, and save the document.

Checking your work so far

You can't preview form interactions in InDesign CC, so you'll do a quick export to Adobe Acrobat Pro to make sure the form is working properly so far.

1 Choose File > Export.

2 For the format, choose Adobe PDF (Interactive), leave the default filename (which should be Subscription Form.pdf) and click Save.

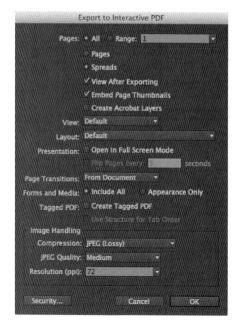

Note: Old or non-Adobe PDF readers may not support form features. For best results, preview forms in the most recent version of Acrobat Pro or Adobe Reader. Adobe Reader is not included with Creative Cloud; it is a separate free download from http://get.adobe.com/reader.

3 In the Export to Interactive PDF dialog box, make sure View After Exporting is selected, and make sure Include All is selected in the Forms and Media section.

4 Leave the other settings at the default and click OK. InDesign exports the PDF document and opens it in Acrobat XI Pro

5 Click the radio buttons and the check box you added to make sure they work. Only one of the radio buttons should be selected at anytime, and you should be able to click to toggle the check box on and off.

Note: Acrobat highlights form objects by default to make them easier to see. To see a PDF form without highlighting the fields, deselect the Highlight Existing Fields button in the purple form toolbar at the top of the Acrobat window.

6 When you're done, close the PDF file without saving changes, and switch back to InDesign.

If you leave the PDF file open, it may prevent InDesign from replacing it when you later export an updated PDF file.

Adding text fields

Adding text entry fields into an InDesign form is as easy as drawing a rectangle, because you can convert a selected rectangle to a text field. You'll do this to build most of the two middle sections of the form. Fortunately, you can duplicate text fields, which will save you work.

1   With the Rectangle tool (), draw a rectangle inside and slightly smaller than the table cell to the right of the First Name label. The exact size isn't important yet because you'll precisely adjust the size in the next step.

2   With the rectangle selected, deselect the "Constrain proportions for width & height" button in the Control panel, enter **20p** into the W (Width) field, enter **1p2** into the H (Height) field, and press Enter/Return.

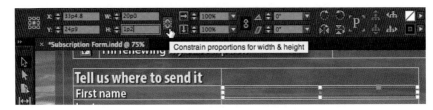

3   In the Swatches panel, set the fill color to Paper and the stroke color to None to customize the appearance of the rectangular text field.

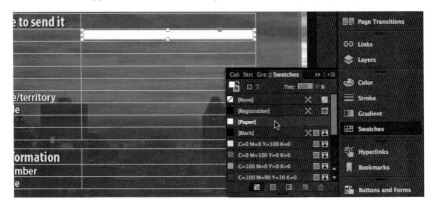

Given the colored background of this form design, a white fill color helps keep the text fields legible, even if the form is printed and filled out by hand.

4 With the rectangle selected, in the Buttons and Forms panel choose Text Field from the Type menu. This converts the rectangle from a simple graphic to a functional form field, indicated by a dashed outline that appears around the field.

5 Near the bottom of the Buttons and Forms panel, select the Required check box in the PDF Options group.

If some form fields are not optional, you can mark them as Required. By default, Acrobat Pro outlines required PDF form fields in red.

The new text field is currently positioned independently on the layout. Now you'll paste it into a table cell as you did earlier with the radio buttons and check box, because you're using the table to align the form objects.

6 With the Selection tool, select the rectangle and choose Edit > Cut.

7 With the Type tool, click an insertion point in the table cell to the right of the First Name label and choose Edit > Paste.

8 Save the document and repeat steps 1–4 in the section "Checking your work so far" to export another draft of the PDF form. If you get a warning that Subscription Form.pdf already exists, click the Replace button.

Note: If the export fails because you get a warning about permission issues or the file being in use, first make sure the previous PDF draft isn't still open in Acrobat. If that doesn't work, try quitting Acrobat, and also try deleting the previous PDF draft.

9 In Acrobat, type a name into the First Name field you created.

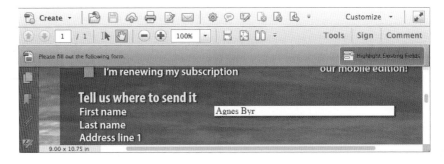

The field should work fine, but the text may be slightly large for the field. In the figure above, the descenders of some letters may be cut off. Before you create the rest of the text fields, you'll resolve this issue.

10 Close the PDF file without saving changes, and return to InDesign.

11 With the Selection tool, select the rectangle, and in the Buttons and Forms panel choose Auto from the Font Size menu.

The Auto option resizes text so that it's always completely visible inside a text field. However, if a large amount of text is entered into a small field, the text may become very small. With the short bits of text that will be entered into these fields, that should not be a problem.

Now you'll finish off the rest of the text fields.

Using appropriate form objects

Each choice you have for form objects has a specific purpose, so it's best to choose the appropriate type. Here's how to pick the right form object for the job:

- A button is best used to initiate an action, such as playing a video or submitting a form.
- A check box group represents options that aren't mutually exclusive: You can pick more than one. For example, you could use check boxes to let users indicate which countries they have visited.
- A radio button represents options that are mutually exclusive: You can pick only one. For example, you could use radio buttons to let someone indicate the country in which they were born. You wouldn't want to use check boxes for this purpose because it would allow users to select multiple countries of birth, which would be invalid.
- A list box presents a scrolling list of options. You can allow multiple selections in a list box.
- A combo box presets a drop-down menu of items from which you can select only one. Also, a combo box allows direct text entry.
- A signature field lets someone enter a digital signature using a stylus or tablet.
- A text field allows entry of text.

If a form object has options, you'll find them in the Buttons and Forms panel when the object is selected.

12 With the Selection tool, highlight the rectangle and choose Edit > Copy.

13 With the Type tool, click an insertion point in the table cell to the right of the Last Name label and choose Edit > Paste.

14 Repeat step 13 for the subsequent table cells, pasting the last text field to the right of the Expiration Date label.

> **Tip:** In form fields that are large enough onscreen, an icon in the bottom-right corner indicates the field type when InDesign is in Normal viewing mode.

Tell us where to send it	
First name	
Last name	
Address line 1	
Address line 2	
City	
State/province/territory	
Zip/postal code	
Country	
Email address	
Payment information	
Credit card number	
Expiration date	

Creating combo boxes

A combo box makes it possible to enter data either by typing it in as you would with a text field or by choosing from a list of values in a drop-down menu. This combination of functions makes the combo box a useful type of form object. You'll add a couple of combo boxes to simplify the entry of the month and the year of the credit card expiration date. You'll use the last pasted text field as a starting point.

1 With the Selection tool, select the rectangle text field you pasted to the right of the Expiration Date label.

2 In the Control panel, enter **3p** into the W (width) field, and press Enter/Return.

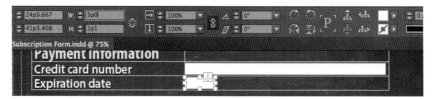

3 With the rectangle still selected, in the Buttons and Forms panel choose Combo Box from the Type menu.

Now you'll create a list of months from 01 to 12.

4 Enter **01** in the List Items option that appears at the bottom of the Buttons and Forms panel, and click the + button or press Enter/Return. Repeat for **02**, **03**, and so on until you get to **12**.

5 With the Type tool, click to the right of the month combo box you just created and type a slash character (/). This is the slash that typically appears between the month and year.

6 With the Selection tool, select the month combo box and choose Edit > Copy.

7 With the Type tool, click an insertion point in the table cell to the right of the slash and choose Edit > Paste.

Now you'll create a list of the next few years.

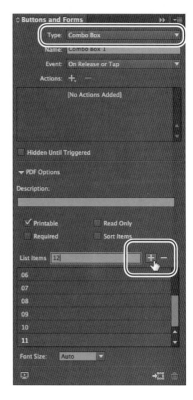

8 With the Selection tool, click the rectangle you just pasted, select the 01 list item in the Buttons and Forms panel, and click the minus (−) button to remove all of the months from the list.

9 As you did in step 4, create a list, but this time have the series go from **2014** to **2020**. Although you had to re-create the list, copying the other combo box still took less time than drawing and setting up another combo box form field from scratch.

▶ **Tip:** You can change the order of a form object's list by dragging the items up or down.

10 Save the document and export another version to PDF.

11 In Acrobat, try out the text fields and the combo boxes you just made.

12 Because this is just a test, close the PDF document without saving changes. Then return to InDesign.

Finishing the form objects

The table holding the form elements could use some tidying up. But first you'll finish the set of radio buttons at the bottom of the form, as well as the submission button.

1 With the Type tool, highlight the radio button next to "$1 an issue…" at the top of the form, and choose Edit > Copy.

2 With the Type tool, click an insertion point in the table cell next to the Phone App label near the bottom of the form, and choose Edit > Paste.

3 With the Selection tool, select the radio button you just pasted, and in the Buttons and Forms panel, change the name to **Discovery** and press Enter/Return.

Changing the name is necessary because you're starting a different group of radio buttons. If all radio buttons on a page had the same name, selecting one radio button would deselect all other radio buttons on the page, so assign one name to each group of radio buttons.

4 With the Type tool, highlight the radio button you just renamed, and copy and paste it into the other seven cells at the bottom of the form as shown.

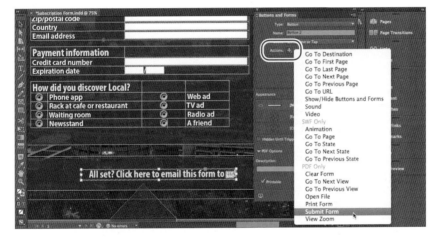

The last item to make interactive is the text field at the very bottom of the page.

5 With the Selection tool, select the text frame containing the text "All set? Click here to email..."

6 In the Buttons and Forms panel, choose Button from the Type menu.

7 In the Buttons and Forms panel, click the plus sign menu next to the Actions label and choose Submit Form.

Normally, the next step would be to enter a path in the URL field, which would lead to a web server that is set up to receive the data in this form, but for this lesson you'll omit that step.

8 Save the document and export another version to PDF.

9 In Acrobat, try clicking the text button you just made. Because you didn't enter a URL the button won't lead to a website. If a security warning alert appears, click Cancel.

10 Because this is just a test, close the PDF document without saving changes. Then return to InDesign.

Cleaning up the table containing the form

You've probably noticed that the table headings aren't all aligned. You'll tidy up the table before you export the final version.

1   Drag the Type tool down the three cells containing the radio buttons and the check box, and in the Control panel, click the Align Left button.

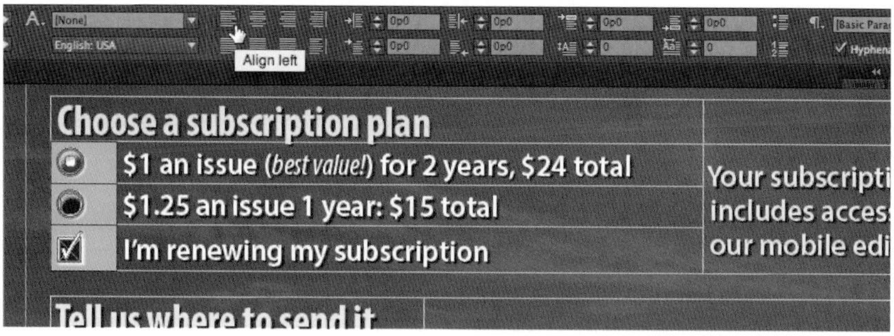

2   Position the pointer over the vertical cell border next to the three cells you just aligned, and drag to the left to remove the extra space.

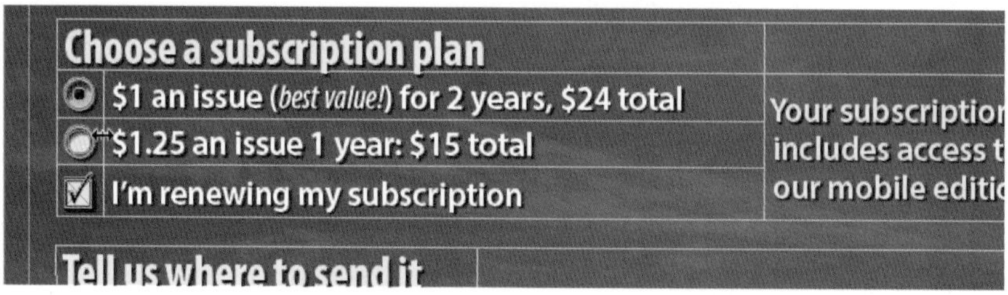

3   In the table containing the "How did you discover Local?" radio button group, align the radio buttons and adjust the vertical cell borders until they are more consistent, similar to step 2 and as shown in the following figure.

Now the headings are all aligned and are no longer too long for their cells.

4   Save the document and export another version to PDF.

5 In Acrobat, try out the text fields and the combo boxes you just made. When you click the "All set? Click here..." link you set up at the bottom of the form, it will produce a warning; click Cancel. It is currently not set up to do anything, but in a real form it would be set up to submit the form data to an actual web server.

▶ **Tip:** To let users of Adobe Reader 8 and later save data they enter into your PDF form, open it in Acrobat Pro and choose File > Save As > Reader Extended PDF > Enable Additional Features. Click Save Now in the dialog box that appears, and then save it under a new name.

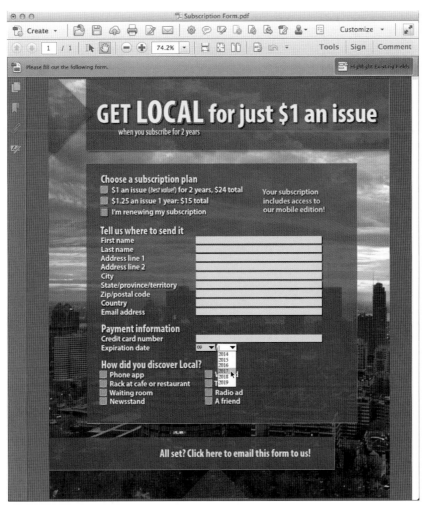

6 Close the PDF document without saving changes, and return to InDesign.

7 Close the InDesign document, and if you're asked if you want to save changes, click Save.

Throughout this lesson you haven't been saving changes to the PDF document because you've only been testing the form. Saving changes to a PDF form is necessary when you're entering data that you want to keep. A form recipient would want to save the changes.

Wrapping up

You've learned how to use the tools in InDesign CC to create an interactive PDF form that people can open and fill out using the free Adobe Reader or Acrobat Pro XI. Now you can create forms that take advantage of the powerful design tools in InDesign so that your forms can be visually compelling, fully functional, and easy for people to fill out.

Review questions

1 Why is it important to consult with your web developer before designing a form?

2 What's the main difference between radio buttons and check boxes?

3 Why do some of the sample form objects have three versions?

4 If selecting a radio button deselects all other radio buttons in other button groups instead of only within the same group, how do you fix it?

5 If a recipient is not able to fill out a PDF form, what could potentially resolve the issue?

Review answers

1 When a form is submitted electronically, the form field data must be formatted properly for the database that will receive it.

2 You can make only one selection from a group of radio buttons, but you can make multiple selections from a group of check boxes.

3 Form objects can support multiple visual states, so that the object can look different depending on whether it's on or off, or the pointer is over it.

4 All buttons within a radio button group must use the same name, but the button name of each group must be different. If buttons are switching on and off in other groups, some buttons may be using a name of another button group.

5 Make sure the recipient is using a recent version of Acrobat Pro or Adobe Reader, because older versions or non-Adobe software that reads PDF files may not fully support form features.

9 PREPARING IMAGES FOR MULTIPLE MEDIA

Lesson overview

In this lesson you'll learn how to intelligently prepare and manage images for use across different media:

- Understanding the multiple meanings of resolution and how they apply to different media

- Adjusting image size as you crop

- Sharpening images for different media

- Preparing image color for different media

- Inspecting and changing image resolution in various Adobe software applications

 You'll probably need between one and two hours to complete this lesson. Download the project files for this lesson from the Lesson & Update Files tab on your Account page at www.peachpit.com and store them on your computer in a convenient location, as described in the "Getting Started" section of this book. Your Accounts page is also where you'll find any updates to the chapters or to the lesson files. Look on the Lesson & Update Files tab to access the most current content.

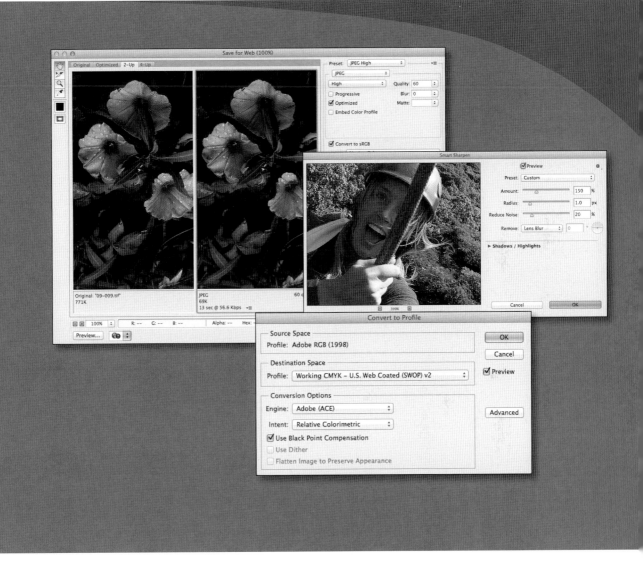

Learn how to optimize the size, resolution, and color
of a source image so that it reproduces well in print,
on the web, and on mobile devices.

Note: If you have not already downloaded the project files for this lesson to your computer from your Account page, make sure you do so now. See "Getting Started" at the beginning of the book.

One image, multiple paths

An image today can be reproduced in many different ways. Unlike the time when an image's only destiny was to be printed on a press, now an image can also be shown on a website or displayed in a video. These media have very different reproduction requirements, so if you want your images to look their best, use Adobe Creative Cloud tools to properly optimize versions of an image for different media. For example, it's important to prepare images for a website at a file size that's appropriate for the connection speed of the site's audience so that the website loads quickly. Preparing images in the correct color space helps ensure that image colors stay as consistent as possible throughout different types of output.

When you prepare an image for output on only one device, such as a printing press, you can simply edit the image as needed and archive it when the job is done. But when you know an image will be used in multiple media, you need to do a little more advance planning. Every output device—from a press to a smartphone to an inkjet printer—has its own capabilities and limitations, so optimizing an image for one specific device may cause it to work less well on other devices. For example, if you convert an RGB image to CMYK color for a printing press, and then later create a copy of that CMYK image for the web, its colors may appear dull compared to if you had created a web version from the original RGB image. Similarly, taking a low-resolution image from a website and printing it on a printing press may result in a coarse-looking image due to inadequate resolution. In both cases, the best solution is to produce each media-specific version from the original, or master, image. The master image can be a camera raw image or a digital negative (DNG) file if all necessary corrections were completed in Adobe Camera Raw, or it can be a layered Photoshop document containing your edits. If the image is a graphic drawn from scratch, it can also be an Adobe Illustrator (AI) document.

Adobe Creative Cloud applications are designed to help you optimize images for different media. You can use Adobe Photoshop or Adobe Illustrator to easily export a web-optimized duplicate of an image that leaves the master (original) image untouched.

Image resolution and media

The number of pixels you send to a printer or a screen affects your production efficiency and your viewer's experience. Send an image with too few pixels and the image looks coarse and blocky. Send too many pixels and downloading, viewing, and printing will be slow. Fortunately, Adobe Creative Cloud applications provide ways to inspect and adjust resolution while preserving quality.

Understanding the multiple meanings of resolution

In digital design, the term resolution is used in different ways:

- **As pixel dimensions, such as 1024 x 768 pixels.** This is typically used for onscreen media, such as web and video, as well as for cameras. You'll probably also recognize this usage from the specifications for computer and video displays; for example, 1920 x 1080 pixels is the display size for 1080p HD televisions. But pixel dimensions alone tell you nothing about the actual displayed size of an image; for example, a 1920 x 1080-pixel HDTV can be 27 inches or 60 inches (measured diagonally) in size.

- **As a ratio expressing the density of dots on a display or in print, such as 300 pixels per inch.** Expressing resolution as a ratio has traditionally been associated with printed output, but it's becoming more common in discussions of displays such as tablets and smartphones as their pixel density approaches that of print, for instance the 326 ppi display of the iPhone 5. Because pixels per inch is a ratio, expressing resolution this way requires two values: a dimension in pixels and a physical measurement such as inches. For example, 3000 pixels along 10 inches equals 300 pixels per inch.

- **As megapixels.** This is simply the number of pixels in an image expressed in millions of pixels; 1 megapixel is 1 million pixels. You usually see resolution expressed as megapixels in the specifications for digital cameras. Megapixels are directly related to the pixel dimensions of the images produced by a digital camera, so it's easy to work out the megapixel resolution of any image. For example, to determine how many megapixels are in a digital camera image that's 4500 x 3000 pixels, simply multiply the two dimensions: 4500 times 3000 equals 13,500,000 pixels, or 13.5 megapixels. Because megapixels represent pixel dimensions only, they do not indicate pixel density until you specify the physical size of the image (such as 10 inches).

In conversation, these different meanings for resolution can cause confusion, so keep these differences in mind as you work in various media. Later in this lesson you'll learn how to inspect images for pixel dimensions and density.

▶ **Tip:** The abbreviations ppi (pixels per inch) and dpi (dots per inch) are both used to describe resolution as pixel density. Generally, ppi is used when measuring pixels (picture elements) in an image file or on a monitor, whereas dpi is generally used when referring to dots on printed output.

Typical media resolutions

As you prepare images for various media, what resolutions should you aim for? This overview provides some guidelines for sizing images for various media, and later in this lesson you'll adjust an image to various media sizes.

Online media

When you're designing for onscreen media, such as websites, video programs, or mobile devices, you'll want to determine the space available to the image in the design as expressed in pixel dimensions. In conventional web design, the pixel dimensions of a web page are based on the pixel dimensions of the typical display used by the target audience, and the pixel dimensions of individual images are designed to fit within that layout. For example, a web designer might design based on an assumption that a site will be viewed mostly on netbook displays that are 1024 pixels wide.

However, that practice is rapidly changing as more sites accommodate mobile devices, which have a wide range of screen sizes. Several years ago most displays were on a desktop or laptop computer and ranged between 15 and 17 inches. Today, display sizes span 3-inch smartphones, 10-inch tablets, 15-inch laptops, and 27-inch desktop monitors. In addition, screen resolutions are rapidly increasing. In the past it was always assumed that screen resolutions were always far lower than print resolutions. Many new devices use displays that exceed a print-like 300 pixels per inch; these displays are often referred to as Retina or HiDPI displays. This means that images you prepare for apps or websites that support Retina/HiDPI displays may contain as many pixels as a print image.

Video projects, such as the kind you can create in Adobe Photoshop, still use fixed frame sizes. If you want an image to fill the screen, determine the pixel dimensions of the video standard, and then resize or crop the image as needed. For example, if you're creating a 720p HD video, you should create images that match the 1280 x 720 pixel dimensions of that video standard.

Printed media

The resolution requirements for printed media are not always straightforward. Just because an inkjet printer creates output at 2880 dpi does not mean you should save images at 2880 ppi; in fact, it's very unlikely that you would because most printing technologies create colors and tones by combining printer dots into larger cells or patterns. In general, you'll find the following guidelines to be helpful:

- For general office use or for documents you'll photocopy, it's usually best to use image resolutions between 150 and 300 ppi.

- For prepress or fine-art printing, images are typically reproduced at 240 to 360 dpi. However, the more expensive the job, the more you'll want to consult with your prepress service provider before committing to the job to find out which resolution you should target when preparing images based on the specific printing system your service provider uses.

- Viewing distance can affect resolution requirements. For example, a roadside billboard or large banner can be printed at 100 dpi because it won't be seen up close. An image's pixel density of 150 dpi at arm's length becomes an effective pixel density of 300 dpi simply by doubling the viewing distance. Your service provider can advise you on the optimum resolution for the printing medium and viewing distance of your job.

▶ **Tip:** For any online medium, remember to increase the pixel dimensions of an image if the image will be magnified, so that it still appears detailed after it's enlarged. For example, if you expect a 1080p video project to zoom into an image 200%, instead of creating a 1920 x 1080 pixel image, scale each dimension by 200% to produce a 3840 x 2160 pixel image.

▶ **Tip:** For prepress output, you may hear the term lines per inch or lpi, also called a screen frequency or screen ruling. This is a different value than dpi or ppi, and describes the number of lines of halftone cells per inch. Halftone cells are a method for creating the illusion of gray shades or color tints using solid ink, and each cell is built out of multiple printer dots. For example, you may be asked to provide 300 dpi images for 150 lpi output on a 2400 dpi imagesetter.

Image color and media

Different media have varying color requirements:

- Online media uses color specified using the RGB color mode, either as RGB values (such as red 108, green 18, and blue 172) or a hexadecimal value (#6c12ac).

- Printed media intended for a press typically uses color specified using the CMYK color mode (such as cyan 72%, magenta 95%, yellow 0%, black 0%).

- Although printing ink is typically based on the CMYK color mode, some printing processes may expect to receive color specified using the RGB color mode if the conversion to CMYK will happen after the job is sent to the printer, for example, when colors are converted by the printer driver behind the scenes. This is the case with most desktop inkjet printers and some on-demand presses.

Within a color mode, multiple color spaces are possible. Color spaces are variations commonly based on the particular color range that a display or print device can actually reproduce. You can read a more complete explanation of color management (available on your Accounts page at Peachpit.com), but for this lesson, you'll convert online RGB colors to the sRGB color space, which is a standard for the web and computer monitors. You'll also convert print colors to a generic CMYK color space—although for an actual print job you'd convert CMYK color to the color space of a specific press standard.

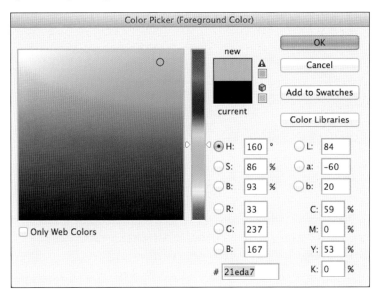

The color picker in Adobe Photoshop lets you specify color values in different color modes, including HSB (Hue, Saturation, Brightness), RGB, hexadecimal for the web, and CMYK.

Preparing graphics for the web or mobile devices

Now you'll prepare an image for online media. The image starts out as a DNG (digital negative) file from a digital camera. You'll make the necessary corrections to size, resolution, and color.

Exporting images for online media using only Adobe Bridge and Adobe Camera Raw

For this part of the lesson, you'll start with a set of photos and create versions for a website. The website requires the photos to be 1000 pixels along the longest side.

1   In Adobe Bridge, navigate to the Lesson09 folder in your Lessons folder.

2   Select the file Beach.dng.

3   If the Metadata panel isn't visible, choose Window > Metadata Panel.

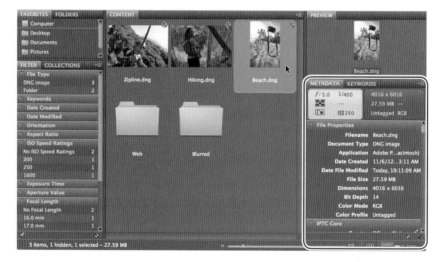

In the File Properties section in the Metadata panel, note the Dimensions, Color Mode, and Color Profile sections. The Dimensions are the pixel dimensions, the Color Mode is RGB, and the Color Profile is "Untagged" because it's a Camera Raw file. The Bit Depth is 14 bits per channel, which is the bit depth at which the camera captured the images. You can use the Metadata panel in Adobe Bridge to check file specifications without opening them.

Now you'll take the steps necessary to meet the specifications from the website.

4 Select the three images in the Lesson09 folder, and choose File > Open in Camera Raw (Ctrl-R/Command-R).

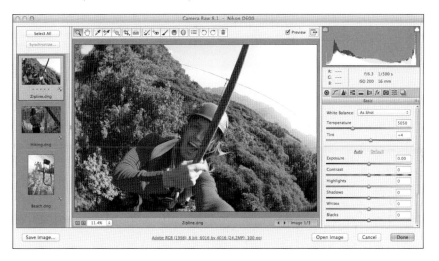

The files open in Camera Raw, and you see all three in a filmstrip along the left side of the Camera Raw dialog box.

This lesson concentrates on the production aspects of the image, not basic image correction, so you won't make other adjustments in Camera Raw. You'll set up options that affect the conversion to Photoshop and then proceed directly to Photoshop.

5 Click the underlined link text at the bottom of the Camera Raw dialog box.

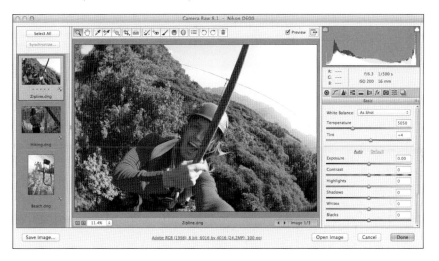

6 In the Workflow Options dialog box that appears, make the following settings that are appropriate for web output:

- For Space, choose sRGB IEC61966-2.1.

- For Depth, choose 8 Bits/Channel.

- For Image Sizing, select Resize to Fit, choose Long Side, enter **1000** and choose Pixels, and leave Resolution unchanged (it should read 300 pixels/ inch). Leaving Resolution at 300 ppi will not affect web output, as you will see.

> ▶ **Tip:** When you choose a different color space in the Workflow Options dialog box, notice that the histogram changes. The reason is that the Camera Raw histogram represents the distribution of colors in the currently selected color space.

- In the Output Sharpening section, select the Sharpen For option, choose Screen from the Sharpen For menu, and choose Standard from the Amount menu.

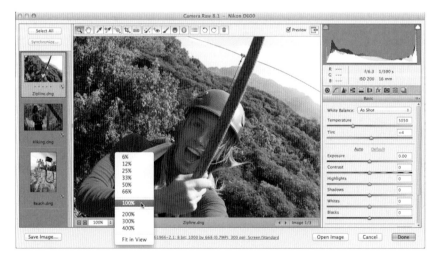

7 Click OK to close the Workflow Options dialog box. The image may now look blocky because it maintained the size of the image on the screen even though the number of pixels was significantly reduced. You can change the view magnification in Camera Raw to display one image pixel for each screen pixel.

8 Choose 100% from the magnification menu below the bottom-left corner of the preview.

The changes you make in the Workflow Options dialog box don't alter the original raw files. Although Camera Raw displays a preview of the Workflow Options settings, the settings are applied only to the copies of the raw files that Camera Raw generates when you convert to another format, as you will in the next steps or when you open the raw files in Photoshop.

Note: In Camera Raw, image editing settings are saved with each image, but Workflow Settings are saved only for Camera Raw, not with individual images.

1 Click the Select All button at the top of the filmstrip.

2 Click the Save Images button, and in the Save Options dialog box, do the following:

- Click the Select Folder button and set the Destination to the Web folder in your Lesson09 folder.

- For File Naming, choose Document Name for the first field, and enter **_web** for the second field.

- For Format, choose JPEG. Notice that this automatically sets the File Extension field in the File Naming section.

- For Metadata, choose Copyright & Contact Info Only. This is a good choice if you want to hide shot data, keywords, and other metadata but preserve ownership and licensing information.

- For Quality, choose High (8-9).

3 Click Save to close the Save Options dialog box. A progress indicator appears next to the Save Images button to let you know how many images remain to be processed.

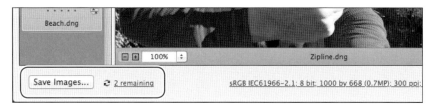

4 Click Done.

5 In the Lesson09 folder in Adobe Bridge, select the Beach_web.jpg image you just saved.

6 In the Metadata panel, notice that the Dimension of each of the new JPEG files is limited to 1000 pixels on its long side and the Color Profile is sRGB, both because of your Workflow Options settings.

7 Press the left arrow key or right arrow key to view the other images and their metadata, which should be consistent with the settings you made in the Camera Raw Workflow Options dialog box.

▶ **Tip:** Adobe Camera Raw can process TIFF and JPEG files as well as camera raw files.

The ability of Camera Raw to edit images, set output options, and then output resized and sharpened images directly from Camera Raw means that in many cases you may not need to continue on to Photoshop before creating images that are ready for final output.

You might also have noticed that the Resolution setting in Workflow Options was left at 300 ppi, and yet this did not affect the onscreen image size in any way. The reason is that websites and mobile devices don't typically use a ppi or dpi resolution value to set the size of the image. On the web, image size is set by the pixel dimensions of an image or by web page code that positions and scales the image. (The latter is more likely for websites optimized for Retina or HiDPI displays.)

Exporting images for online media using Photoshop

In the previous example, you optimized images using Adobe Camera Raw without entering Photoshop. Of course, there are times when you'll need to make corrections that can be achieved only with Photoshop. In the following example you'll save a currently unusable image by using the Shake Reduction feature in Photoshop, and then you'll reduce its dimensions to 500 pixels wide as you save an optimized copy for the web from Photoshop.

1 In Adobe Bridge, navigate to the Blurred folder in your Lesson09 folder, select the file Flower.psd, and press Enter/Return. The file opens in Photoshop; if Photoshop isn't already open, it may take a few seconds to start up.

Note: Pressing Enter/Return in Adobe Bridge is the same as choosing File > Open, which opens the selected files in their default applications. You can set those in the File Type Associations panel in the Preferences dialog box in Adobe Bridge.

This image contains a significant amount of blur because it was taken at a slow shutter speed and the camera moved during the exposure. You can use the Shake Reduction feature in Photoshop to help make the image usable. Shake Reduction is not available in Camera Raw, so it's a good example of an edit that would require Photoshop. Although Camera Raw does provide sharpening tools, they are designed to sharpen details that are assumed to be stationary. The motion blur that results from camera shake typically exists along an irregular path traced by the shake.

2 Choose Filter > Sharpen > Shake Reduction.

The Shake Reduction dialog box may take a few seconds to analyze the image, calculate the correction, and display it. Image sharpness should be significantly improved.

▶ **Tip:** Pressing P to toggle the preview on and off works in most Photoshop dialog boxes that have a Preview check box.

3 Deselect the Preview option (press P) to see how the image looked before the Shake Reduction correction, and then reselect Preview (or press P again) to restore the preview of the corrected image.

4 Although the current correction isn't perfect, the image will be exported at half of the current pixel dimensions to fit within a web page layout. To see how it looks at half its current size, choose 50% from the magnification menu at the bottom-left corner of the Shake Reduction window.

At the smaller size, the effect of Shake Reduction should appear quite acceptable compared to the original image because the unsightly artifacts have also been reduced in size.

5   Click the disclosure triangle next to the Advanced heading to expand that section. A dashed rectangle appears around a part of the image. The rectangle represents a Blur Estimation Region. When you open the Shake Reduction dialog box, Shake Reduction automatically determines the initial settings and the Blur Estimation Region.

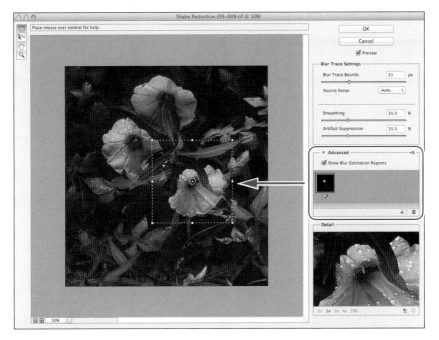

If you think another area of the image better represents the camera shake blur that needs to be corrected, you can drag the center of a Blur Estimation Region to move it to another area or you can drag its handles to resize it. If the nature of the camera shake is not uniform (such as one side of the camera was moved differently than another side), you can also add additional regions. In this case, the automatic result is a sufficient improvement, so you will leave it as is.

6   Click the disclosure triangle next to the Advanced heading to collapse that section. The Blur Estimation Region is now hidden.

7   Click OK to close the Shake Reduction dialog box.

You're now ready to create a version optimized for the web. You may be familiar with using the Save As command to create a new version of a photo in a different format, but for the web it's better to use the Save for Web command because it provides a range of web-specific optimization features.

Tip: You'll also find the Save for Web dialog box in Adobe Illustrator.

1 Choose File > Save for Web.

2 In the Save for Web dialog box, do the following and then click Save:

- Click the 2-Up tab, and choose JPEG High from the Preset menu. Clicking the 2-Up tab lets you compare the original image with a preview of the current optimization settings so you can make sure the image appearance and file size are acceptable. If they aren't, you can change the optimization settings in the top-right corner of the Save for Web dialog box.

- Make sure Convert to sRGB is selected to ensure that whatever the original color space of the image, it will be properly converted for online media.

- In the Image Size section, enter **500** for W (width) and press Tab to apply the value and update the previews. The artifacts that remained after applying Shake Reduction should now be much less visible after reducing the pixel dimensions of the image.

- For Quality choose Bicubic Sharper, which is a scaling method designed to maintain image sharpness that would normally be lost when reducing the size of an image.

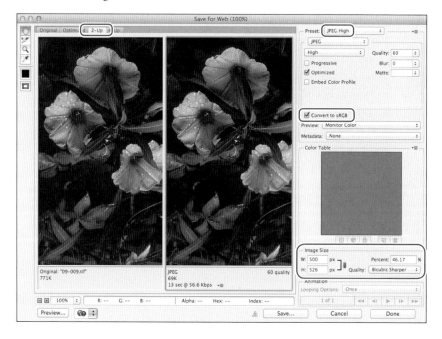

3 Click Save, and in the Save Optimized As dialog box, navigate to your Lesson09 folder and then to the Web folder inside it, name the file **Flower_web.jpg**, and click Save. If you see a compatibility warning about filename characters, click OK to accept it.

4 Close the Photoshop document. When asked if you want to save changes, click Save.

5 Switch to Adobe Bridge, navigate to the Flower_web.jpg file you just saved, and press the spacebar to view it full screen.

You've prepared images for online media in two ways: editing through Camera Raw and editing through Photoshop, and in both cases you used Adobe Bridge to inspect images before editing and to verify them after editing.

Preparing graphics for print

Now you'll prepare a DNG image for a job going to press, making the necessary corrections to size, resolution, and color.

Exporting images for print media using Photoshop

For this part of the lesson, you'll create a graphic that needs to be 2 inches wide and 3 inches tall to fit in a page layout for printed output. The original is horizontal, so you'll use Photoshop to crop the image to the layout specifications.

1 In Adobe Bridge, select the file Zipline.dng in the Lesson09 folder in your Lessons folder, and press Enter/Return to open it in Camera Raw hosted by Photoshop.

2 Click the underlined link text at the bottom of the Camera Raw dialog box.

3 In the Workflow Options dialog box that appears, do the following:

- For Space, choose Adobe RGB, which is similar to the range of colors in the CMYK color mode into which the image will be converted later in Photoshop.

- For Depth, choose 16 Bits/Channel.

- Deselect Resize to Fit because you'll be cropping to specific dimensions in Photoshop.

- Set Resolution to **300** pixels/inch.

Note: Although you can also change the photo dimensions using the Image > Image Size command, changing them in Save for Web lets you change only the dimensions of the web version so that you can preserve the image dimensions of the original.

Tip: Another way to test a web image you just exported is to drag it from Adobe Bridge (or from the desktop) into a web browser window.

- Deselect the Sharpen For check box because you should sharpen after performing Photoshop edits.

- Leave the Open in Photoshop as Smart Objects option deselected.

4 Click OK to close the Workflow Options dialog box.

As in the earlier example for online media, this lesson concentrates on the production aspects of the image, not basic image correction. For this reason you'll proceed directly to Photoshop without making further corrections in Camera Raw.

5 Click Open Image to convert the raw image into Adobe Photoshop format using the settings in the Workflow Options dialog box.

6 If the rulers aren't visible, choose View > Rulers to display them. If the rulers display in pixel units, right-click/Control-click the rulers and choose Inches from the context menu that appears.

7 Select the Crop tool. In the Options bar, choose W x H x Resolution from the Crop tool options menu, and do the following:

- Enter a Width of **2 in** and a Height of **3 in**.

- Enter a Resolution of **300** px/in.

8 Choose New Crop Preset from the Crop tool options menu. The new preset is named automatically using the settings, so you'll accept the suggested name. Click OK.

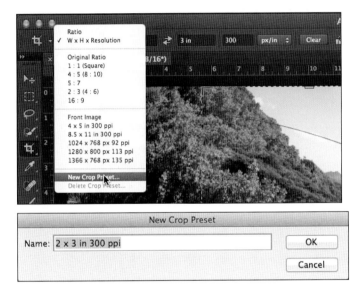

Creating a new crop preset means that if you need to use the Crop tool with the same settings in the future, you can simply choose that preset from the Crop tool options menu.

9 Adjust any side or corner of the crop rectangle to compose the person within the vertical crop rectangle, then drag with the frame to reposition if needed, and then press Enter/Return.

10 When you're done cropping, press Enter/Return until the crop rectangle disappears. The image may now appear small because it's been downsampled from its original full size to the new size.

11 Choose View > 100%.

▶ **Tip:** To permanently display the dimensions of a document in the status bar, click the triangle to the right of the status bar and choose Document Dimensions.

12 Click and hold the mouse on the status bar at the bottom of the document window to confirm that the document dimensions are 2 by 3 inches and the resolution is 300 ppi. The Crop tool accomplished both resizing and setting the resolution in one step.

Now you'll apply sharpening at the current document pixel dimensions and resolution.

13 Choose Filter > Sharpen > Smart Sharpen and do the following:

- Make sure Preview is selected.

- For Amount, enter **150** percent.

- For Radius, enter **1** px.

- For Reduce Noise, enter **20** percent.

- For Remove, choose Lens Blur.

Tip: You can drag any edge of the Smart Sharpen dialog box to enlarge it, which also enlarges the preview.

Feel free to adjust these settings. For example, if you think the Reduce Noise value removes too much detail from the face, lower it slightly.

14 Leave other settings as they are, and click OK to close the Smart Sharpen dialog box.

The image is currently in RGB color mode, which you can verify by viewing the menu that appears when you click the status bar. But the job requires converting the image to CMYK color mode, which you'll do now.

1 Choose Edit > Convert to Profile, and in the Profile menu, choose U.S. Web Coated (SWOP) v2. This option may also appear at the top of the menu as Working CMYK – U.S. Web Coated (SWOP) v2, and you can choose that option as well. Leave the other settings at their defaults, as shown in the following figure. Click OK.

On an actual CMYK print job, it's likely that your prepress service provider would provide a CMYK profile for you to install so that it appears in the Destination Space menu. You would then choose that specific profile instead of the generic one you chose for this lesson. Using a specially tailored CMYK profile helps ensure that colors are converted properly for the specific press on which the job will be printed.

2   Choose Image > Mode > 8 Bits/Channel. Now that all edits and the color conversion are complete, converting the final file from 16 bits per channel to 8 bits per channel creates a more compact file while providing sufficient color range for output on a printing press.

3   Choose File > Save As, navigate to your Lesson09 folder, name the file **Zipline_ CMYK.psd**, and click Save. Close the document window.

Some older workflows may require you to save the image in TIFF format, but Adobe InDesign can directly import Photoshop format (PSD) image files.

Inspecting an image in Adobe InDesign

When you import an image into Adobe InDesign CC, you can easily check its size, resolution, and other attributes as you lay out a document.

1   Start Adobe InDesign CC.

2   Choose File > New > Document.

3   In the New Document dialog box, make sure [Default] is selected as the Document Preset and Print is selected as the Intent, and click OK.

Tip: To navigate into folders in the Mini Bridge panel, double-click them in the folder panel on the left side of the panel.

4   Choose Window > Mini Bridge and navigate to your Lesson09 folder. (If the Launch Bridge button appears in the Mini Bridge panel, click it.)

5 Drag the PSD image you saved into the InDesign layout, and drag the loaded place icon anywhere on the layout to create a graphics frame containing the image. The exact size isn't important.

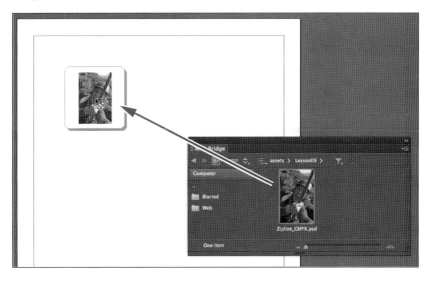

6 With the image selected, notice that there are width (W) and height (H) options in the Control panel at the top of the InDesign workspace. When the Selection tool is active, these options indicate the dimensions of the graphics frame containing the image.

7 With the Selection tool, select the photo.

8 If the Info panel isn't visible, choose Window > Info. It tells you the file type, Actual and Effective ppi, and the image's current color space and color profile.

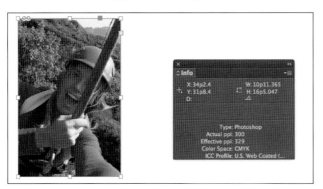

▶ **Tip:** The Info panel displays the color profile of the CMYK image used in this lesson because the profile was set to be embedded in the Save As dialog box in Photoshop. In some CMYK workflows, your prepress service provider may ask you to not embed the CMYK profile, so be sure to ask.

You can use the Control panel or the Info panel to verify the current dimensions of an object on the layout, and you can use the Control panel to resize an image on a layout by entering new dimensions. The Info panel lists Actual and Effective ppi because pixel density on a print layout depends on its physical dimensions on the page. Enlarging lowers the pixel density; reducing increases pixel density.

(If you can't see the ppi readout in the Info panel, make sure the image is selected, and in the Info panel choose Show Options from the Info panel menu. Also, if the Control panel and Info panel are set to a unit of measure other than inches, you can right-click/Control-click the rulers to set them to inches, as you did earlier in Photoshop.)

▶ **Tip:** To view images at full resolution, make sure High Quality Display (View > Display Performance > High Quality Display) is selected. High Quality Display takes more time to redraw, so the three Display Performance options let you balance screen display speed and quality.

9 Ctrl-Shift-drag/Command-Shift-drag any corner handle of the image outward to enlarge the image on the layout. If the image doesn't enlarge, choose Edit > Undo and try again, but this time hold down the two modifier keys before dragging the handle.

▶ **Tip:** Remember that you can use Adobe Bridge to check the specifications of images without having to open or import them into an application.

Notice that in the Info panel the Effective ppi is now lower than the Actual ppi to show that you're stretching the same number of pixels across a larger area, lowering the pixel density. Your prepress service provider can recommend the lowest acceptable Effective ppi for your print job.

When you're getting ready to send out a print job, you don't have to check the specs of each image using the Info panel. The Preflight feature lets you verify all images in the document at once. You used the Preflight feature in Lesson 2.

10 Exit InDesign. When asked if you want to save changes, click Don't Save.

Wrapping up

Well done! You've walked through key steps in properly inspecting and setting image size and resolution for printed and online media using a wide variety of tools available to you as part of your Adobe Creative Cloud subscription.

Review questions

1   What are the three different ways that the term resolution is used in digital media?

2   In Adobe Bridge, which panel is useful for inspecting pixel dimensions, pixel density, and other specifications of a selected image?

3   Why can't the same sharpening settings apply to both online and printed images?

4   When converting image colors to CMYK, which profile is best for printing to a press?

5   In Adobe InDesign, what is the difference between Actual ppi and Effective ppi?

Review answers

1   The term resolution is used when referring to the pixel dimensions of an image or display, the pixel density (ppi or dpi), and camera megapixels.

2   In Adobe Bridge you can use the Metadata panel to inspect image resolution and other specifications for a selected image.

3   The effectiveness of sharpening settings is affected by pixel density, and printed images typically require much higher pixel density than online images.

4   The best CMYK profile to use for a job printed to a press is the profile recommended by your prepress service provider.

5   Actual ppi is the pixel density of the image as it was saved; Effective ppi describes how pixel density is changed after you resize an image on a page layout.

INDEX

EPUB documents. *See also* eBooks
    adding metadata, 252–253
    Adobe Digital Editions, 236
    applying object styles, 248–252
    considerations, 254
    font embedding, 253
    mapping text styles to CSS, 239–240
    page breaks, 240
    previewing final version, 253–254
    rasterizing page layouts, 244–248, 251
    table of contents, 254
EPUB format
    considerations, 241
    described, 241
    online publishing with, 241
    opening documents in, 237–238
    vs. PDF format, 241
    preparing documents for export,
        239–253
    supported reading devices, 236, 241
EPUB standard, 236
e-readers, 236. *See also* eBooks
errors
    linked files, 80
    live captions, 108
    preflight, 79–80, 120–121
Export as HTML command, 152
exporting. *See also* importing
    documents as PDFs, 122
    EPUB export, 239–253
    forms to Acrobat Pro, 262–263
    graphics for online media, 282–291
    graphics for print media, 291–298
    social media background, 63–64
    video, 200–202

F

Facebook, 13, 14
fades, 186–189
Favorites panel, 22
files. *See also* documents
    adding metadata to, 23
    audio, 211–212
    color labels, 24–25
    DNG, 90, 278, 291–298
    exporting. *See* exporting
    JPEG, 286
    linked. *See* linked files
    managing, 16
    opening in Adobe Bridge, 69, 287

opening in Camera Raw, 89–90
organizing, 172–175
PDF. *See PDF entries*
PSD, 296, 297
ratings, 24
sharing, 12–13
sorting, 172
synchronizing, 13
TIFF, 286, 296
fill colors, 138
Fill proxy, 50
Film & Video preset, 177
Filter By Name field, 163–164
Filter panel, 24
filtering fonts, 163–165
filters
    Blur, 34
    Radial, 91–92
    Sharpen, 288, 295
Flash Professional CC, 18
Flattener Preview panel, 115–117
flattening documents, 115–117
folders, adding to Favorites, 22
Folio Builder panel, 225–228, 231
Folio Overlays panel, 213–215
Folio Producer, 225
Folio Producer Editor, 225
folios
    creating, 225–228
    described, 212
    offline, 226
    previewing, 228–230
    submitting, 225
    video control options, 212–213
    viewing in Adobe Content Viewer, 224,
        225, 228–230
font formats, 156–159
fonts, 154–168
    adding/removing, 163, 167
    choosing, 156–158
    in Creative Cloud, 158–167
    desktop, 156, 159
    embedded, 253
    EPUB documents, 253
    filtering, 163–165
    glyphs, 156
    OpenType, 156, 157, 159
    platform issues, 156
    PostScript, 156, 159
    for printing, 156

Site Settings section, 152
slug area, 82
Smart Guides, 28
Smart Objects, 196, 292
smartphones. *See also* mobile devices
  apps for. *See* apps
  compact menus for, 135–140
  considerations, 157, 206, 254, 279, 280
  phone layout, 135–140, 142, 146
  preparing graphics for, 282–291
  screen orientation, 216–224, 228, 230
  websites on. *See* mobile-friendly websites
social media, background image, 51–64
social networking sites, 14
Sort command, 25
sort order, 25
sound. *See* audio
static HTML, 152
stationery, business, 26–40
still images, 181–184
storage, online, 13
Story Editor window, 114–115
style mapping
  to CSS, 239–240
  Microsoft Word, 97–99
styles
  applying, 100, 139, 147
  CSS, 239–240
  InDesign import and, 97–99
  mapping. *See* style mapping
  paragraph, 100, 139, 147, 239–240
  preserving, 97
synchronizing
  application settings, 17
  files, 13
system fonts, 156, 161
System Fonts menu, 161

T

tables, PDF forms, 264–273
tablets. *See also* mobile devices
  alternate vertical layout, 218–224
  apps for. *See* apps
  considerations, 157, 206, 254, 279, 280
  liquid layouts, 216–218
  screen orientation, 216–224, 228, 230
  websites on. *See* mobile-friendly websites
televisions, 177, 182

templates
  InDesign, 69, 71
  ProSite portfolios, 14
text. *See also* content
  adding to business cards, 35–38
  adding to side bar, 60–61
  entering in InDesign documents, 96
  entering in Photoshop documents, 60
  formatting, 97–99, 100
  importing into InDesign documents, 96–99
  marking up in InDesign documents, 112–115
  pasting, 38
  styles. *See* styles
  tracking changes in InDesign, 112–115
  wrapping around frames, 101
Text tool, 137, 162
Text Wrap panel, 101
threaded frames, 99
TIFF files, 286, 296
timeline, video, 178, 180, 192
Timeline panel, 178, 182–199
title-safe area, 182
Touch App plug-ins, 19
Track Changes panel, 113–115
training videos, 17, 221
transitions, 186–189
transparency, 115–117
TrueType format, 156, 157, 159
tutorials, 17, 221
TVs, 177, 182
Twitter, 13, 14
Twitter background, 51–64
type foundries, 159
Type tool, 38, 96, 100
TypeKit. *See* Adobe TypeKit

U

Undo command, 87, 298
Update Link button, 80
Upload to FTP Host command, 152
URLs, 151, 152

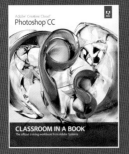

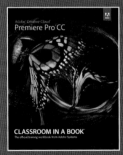